HIDDEN HISTORY *of the* FLORIDA KEYS

Laura Albritton & Jerry Wilkinson

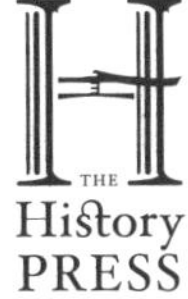

Published by The History Press
Charleston, SC
www.historypress.com

Front cover image courtesy of the Monroe County Public Library, Key West.

First published 2018

Manufactured in the United States

ISBN 9781467138918

Library of Congress Control Number: 2018948029

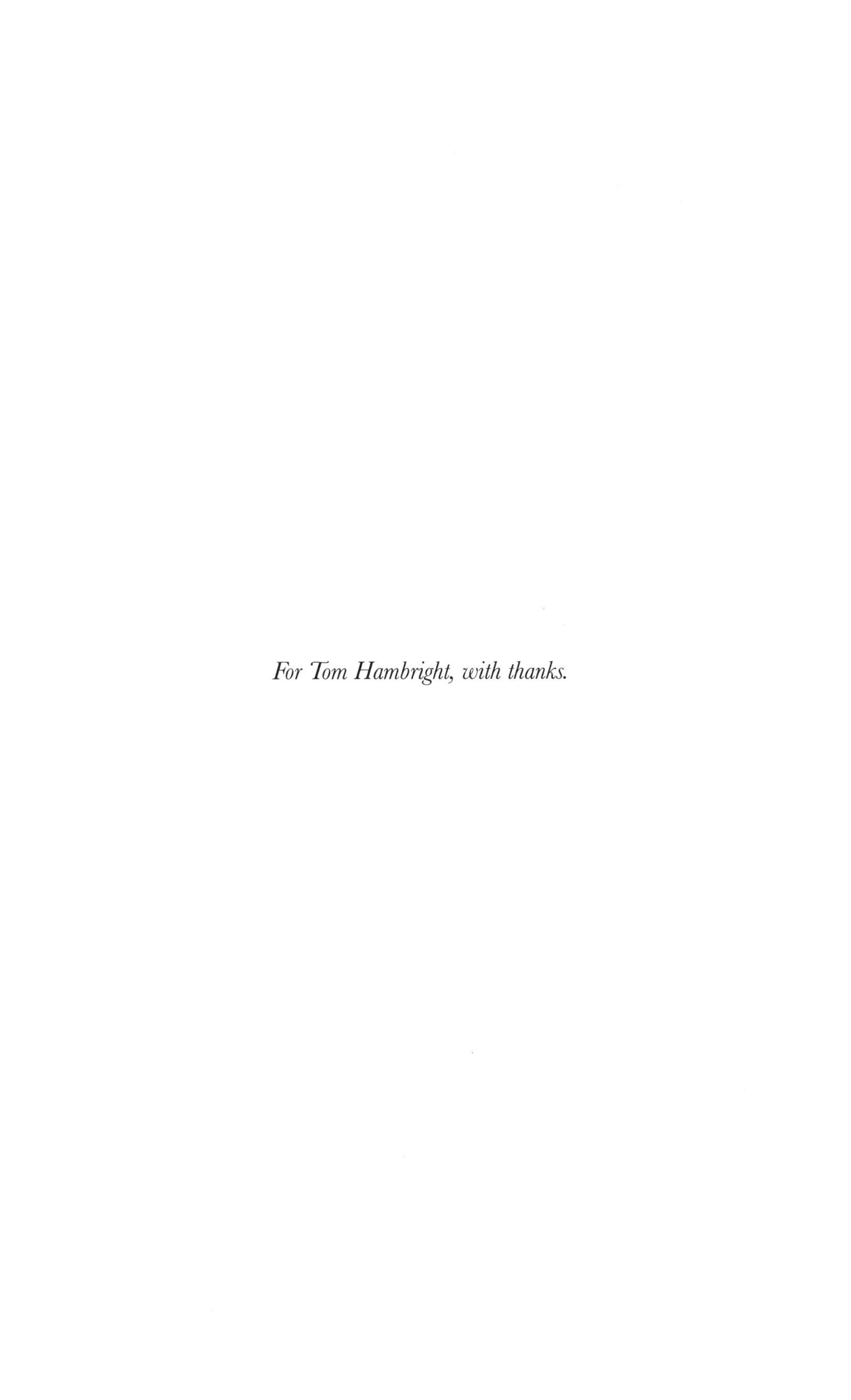

For Tom Hambright, with thanks.

Contents

Acknowledgements

The authors would like to thank historian Tom Hambright and archivist Breana Sowers of the Monroe County Library at Key West for their help in researching this book. Tom provided particularly useful background on the Old Island Restoration Foundation. They are also grateful that they could use several photographs from the Monroe County Library's archive. The assistance of Mark Nicolou, Kathryn Palmer, Jacklyn Attaway and Adam Watson in obtaining research materials and images from the State Archives of Florida was much appreciated. For permission to use images from the Edwin A. and Marion C. Link Collection, they thank the John H. Evans Library at the Florida Institute of Technology and Diane Newman, Special Collections curator. Thanks also go to the Key West Literary Seminar for awarding Laura a writer's residency and to Arlo Haskell and Freya Hendrickson for their kind welcome. Laura also thanks Trudy Hale for a productive writing retreat at the Porches and writer Lisa Hartz for her friendship and encouragement. The authors additionally wish to express their gratitude to everyone at The History Press who made this book possible, including Acquisitions Editors Amanda Irle and Mike Kinsella and Senior Editor Ryan Finn. Last but certainly not least, their most heartfelt gratitude goes out to Zickie Allgrove and Mary Lou Wilkinson.

Introduction

The Florida Keys lie scattered in a graceful arc that extends from the southeast Florida mainland all the way to the Dry Tortugas. At one time, they were remote outposts where seabirds far outnumbered human beings; untouched reefs with brightly colored corals teemed with fish, and dense mangroves lined the shores. While these islands are not especially large (with an area of only 137 square miles), their beauty and the splendor of the surrounding ocean rarely fail to make an impression on those fortunate enough to see them in person. As pioneers from the Americas and Europe began settling here, they transformed the Florida Keys, yet the Keys also transformed them. The obscurity of the location; the unpredictable, tropical weather; and the unique customs and manners that developed over time would mold the settlers into a new breed of Floridian: the Conchs.

From the time of the earliest settlements, Florida Keys history has abounded with outsized adventures, strange events, colorful characters and, of course, natural disasters. It was inevitable that writers and historians would want to chronicle this history, and so they have, in a surprisingly rich abundance of books and articles. This wealth of publication presented the two of us as authors with a conundrum: Could we locate enough "hidden" history to warrant a new book?

Fortunately, one of us (Jerry Wilkinson) has spent decades collecting records, photographs and ephemera that document Florida Keys heritage. Although Jerry has generously shared his expertise in book form, on film, on his extensive website and during hundreds of presentations, there were still episodes he had researched, such as the Key West Extension scare, that could be included in this project. The quest to identify even more hidden history sent another one of us (Laura Albritton) to the Key West library's magical archives to discover stories from the Prohibition era and to investigate the island's early historic preservation movement.

In the end, our book's scope spans 140 years, from the 1820s to the 1960s. In the following ten chapters, you will encounter duelists, soldiers, politicians, pioneers, rumrunners, writers, exotic dancers and historic preservationists. They are, without a doubt, a lively and unusual cast of historic figures. There are vast differences in their backgrounds and socioeconomic situations, not to mention their standards of morality. Nevertheless, the people who lived these stories did have qualities in common: courage, an adventurous spirit and an uncompromising individualism.

Another question emerged as we discussed subjects to cover in the book: Exactly how hidden did these "hidden histories" need to be? Should the history be utterly unheard of or just somewhat lesser known? In the end, we decided to include certain subjects that we hope will surprise even fervent Florida Keys history buffs, in addition to narratives that are less obscure. In some cases, we took subjects that had already been briefly written about (including by ourselves in previous books) and dug further to provide readers with a more detailed understanding of past events. In writing about Adderley Town, in particular, we knew that Marathon residents and Crane Museum visitors would be familiar with the basic story; however, our sense was that outside the Middle Keys, the Adderleys' achievement deserves to be more widely recognized. Finally, in order to make the book accessible to as many readers as possible, we have given historical context and background in each chapter. Whether you have read multiple volumes on Keys history or know next to nothing about the Florida Keys, we hope that you find these ten accounts an illuminating and enjoyable read.

Chapter 1

Pistols at Dawn

On a cool February evening in 1829, Captain Charles Hawkins would have called "good night" to his fellow dinner guests at Ellen Mallory's boardinghouse and lurched out onto the unpaved Key West street. The small town of barely five hundred souls stood hunkered on the northern edge of the island, its house windows illuminated by candlelight and oil lamps. Captain Hawkins most likely carried a torch, for the road was uneven and dark, and especially after such a convivial night, he would have had to watch his step. Little entertainment existed on the remote island outpost, which, as one resident recalled, "naturally led to long sittings over 'the wine cup' at the dinner table of the only general boarding house."[1] One can imagine the captain brushing off his uniform and striding now more confidently toward the snug cottage where he and his wife made their temporary home. Hardly any other face, white or black, would have shown itself on the street at that late hour. The crisp sea air must have felt invigorating after the close quarters of Mrs. Mallory's dining room. Perhaps a small smile played across his lips as he thought of his wife, waiting for him at home. Not a few of the other men at Mrs. Mallory's table must have envied him, with women in Key West in such terribly short supply. A "young thoughtless girl who had seen very little of the world" was how Key West pioneer William Whitehead would describe Mrs. Hawkins decades later.[2]

Something odd about his return home may have made Hawkins suspicious. Perhaps it was the windows of the house that appeared uncharacteristically dark or the fact that his wife did not greet him at the door. "On reaching his

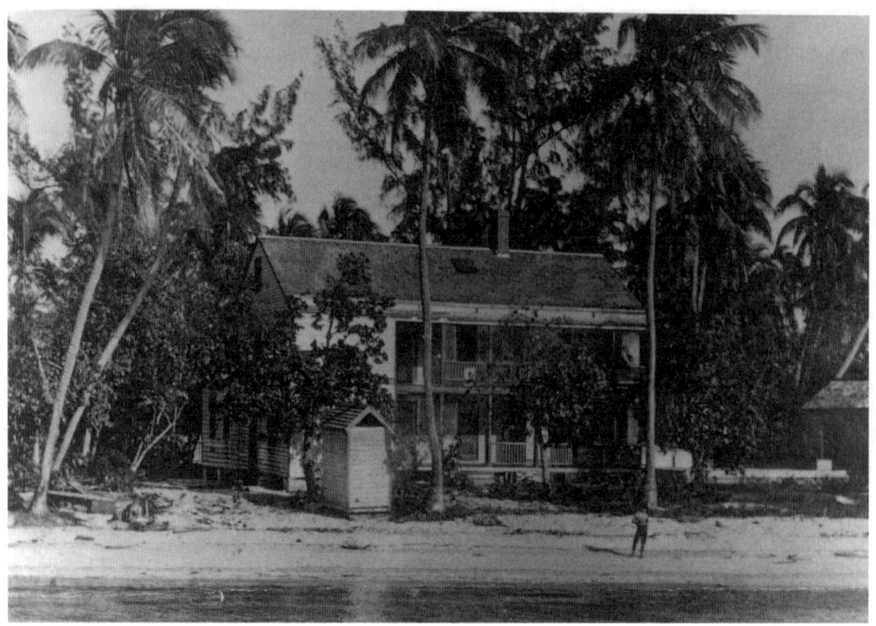

Ellen Mallory's boardinghouse, where Captain Charles Hawkins dined with other Key West residents. *Courtesy of the Monroe County Public Library, Key West.*

house at a late hour," he would have needed to use the torch to see the door latch and let himself inside, where his boots echoed across the sturdy timber floor.[3] He may have spotted a sliver of light spilling through the crack beneath the bedroom door or perhaps the captain heard whispers that intensified his feeling of dread. When he pushed opened the door, Hawkins either saw his young bride fully clothed and nervously darting across the room, or he saw her in her thin, linen chemise and drawers springing off their bed. Whatever clothes she was or was not wearing, Captain Hawkins stared at the open window, where a young man—William Allison McRea, the captain's very own lawyer—was climbing outside.[4] Shock may have momentarily paralyzed him, but not for long. "McRea!" he would have yelled, rushing to intercept him. Grabbing for his pistol and aiming it hurriedly, Hawkins fired.[5]

But it was too late. The young lover had escaped. Peering through the window, the captain would have realized that there was no chance of catching the young man sprinting into the night. What next transpired between husband and wife we can only surmise. Hawkins's temper must have come into play, as he turned on Mrs. Hawkins, possibly shouting, she perhaps sobbing, as he demanded to know what in God's name had she been doing with that scoundrel attorney. The evening, which began so pleasantly for him with the dinner at Ellen Mallory's boardinghouse, would culminate in one of the most disquieting chapters in Florida Keys history.

Captain Charles E. Hawkins was certainly not a man to be trifled with. By 1829, the twenty-seven-year-old officer from New York had already sailed through the Baltic and Mediterranean Seas with the U.S. Navy and served with Commodore David Porter's West Indies Squadron in its battle to rid Florida and Caribbean waters of pirates. As an officer-for-hire, he had done a stint with the naval forces of Colombia. More recently, he sailed under Porter in the service of the Mexican navy.[6] Good looking, tough and prone to a bad temper, he had seen action and knew how to handle himself under fire. William Allison McRea had been acquainted with Hawkins long enough to be aware of the man's background and temperament.

McRea himself had served as the U.S. attorney for the Southern District of Florida. Captain Hawkins held him in high enough regard to hire McRea to represent his interests in legal matters. Nevertheless, one rumor had it that years before, Hawkins and McRea had already crossed swords, literally, in some type of altercation that left Hawkins with "a notable scar across one of his cheeks."[7] Another account, written four decades later, holds that in an effort to repair some friction between them, Captain Hawkins had been giving a dinner in honor of McRea at Ellen Mallory's boardinghouse on *that very night*.[8] (In that case, McRea would have needed to rush like a madman from the dinner to have time to see Mrs. Hawkins.)[9] Whether or not these stories are true, on that breezy, tropical evening in February, one thing was certain: the young buck from Alexandria, Virginia, had made an implacable enemy of Charles Hawkins.

As the sun rose the next morning, momentarily turning the warehouses and wharves of Key West pale shades of rose and tangerine, Captain Charles Hawkins would hardly have been able to contain his impatience. The dazzling colors of the island's sky and surrounding seas must have been matters of complete indifference to the seaman. None of the accounts record precisely what happened next, but we can picture the scene: drawing himself up, tugging on the bottom of his uniform coat, Hawkins may have marched through Key West's dirt roads to the living quarters where McRea resided. We can only speculate how the challenge was made: with a number of passersby as witnesses, did Hawkins slam the flat of his hand against the wood door and bellow, "McRea, I will have satisfaction"? Or the captain may have sent an emissary, who knocked repeatedly on McRea's door until he opened it. One can well imagine the young Virginian appearing in his shirt-sleeves, looking as though he had not slept. McRea may have retorted, "I will defend my honor, sir," or perhaps something less formal and more insulting. One third scenario is that the challenge wasn't delivered in person at all but instead posted publicly on a placard, as had been done in other parts of Florida, demanding satisfaction over this matter of injured honor. (The authorities would not necessarily intervene if Hawkins advertised this publicly—although not technically legal, dueling was often tolerated in Florida, particularly if no one was killed.)

In any event, the two sides reached an agreement on the terms of the duel: pistols, on the morning of the ninth, on the beachfront to the south. Despite the captain's experience fighting at sea, McRea in all likelihood carried himself as if all the odds lay in his own favor. "Cocky" and "brash" would be fitting descriptions for the Virginian. In fact, this would not be the young man's first duel fought over a woman. In Tallahassee, he and a fellow attorney with the unlikely name of Algernon Thruston challenged each other to a duel for Elizabeth Duval's affections. Not only was Elizabeth attractive, but she was also the daughter of Florida's territorial governor, William Pope Duval. In the contest, Thruston managed to wound McRea in the leg, while he himself emerged unscathed. Despite (or perhaps because of) this show of machismo, Elizabeth Duval decided that she wanted nothing to do with either man.[10]

On the morning of February 9, 1829, Hawkins and McRea appeared with their seconds on the beach at the south end of the island. All the noise and activity of the wharves and streets remained at a good distance to the north (near today's Mallory Square). In that era, trees stood where mansions and gracious homes stand today, and the only intruders would have been water birds poking through reeds. A fellow officer from the Mexican navy, one Captain C.C. Hopner, stood ready to offer his friend Hawkins assistance. McRea's second, or "friend," for the duel was a physician, one Dr. R.A. Lacy.[11] (Having a doctor to stand by during a duel would be a shrewd choice, in case of injury.) Their seconds ensured that the men's single-barreled pistols functioned properly, for this was not the moment for one to jam or misfire. Now it was time. The two men walked a set number of paces apart and then drew their pistols. McRea most likely tried to appear unconcerned, even cavalier, while Hawkins had no interest in disguising the hatred that roiled underneath his uniform's coat.

In the still Key West morning, both men pulled their triggers. Their shots rang forth almost simultaneously. The duelists then reached for their second pistol and, once again, shot at each other. Then they reloaded. All told,

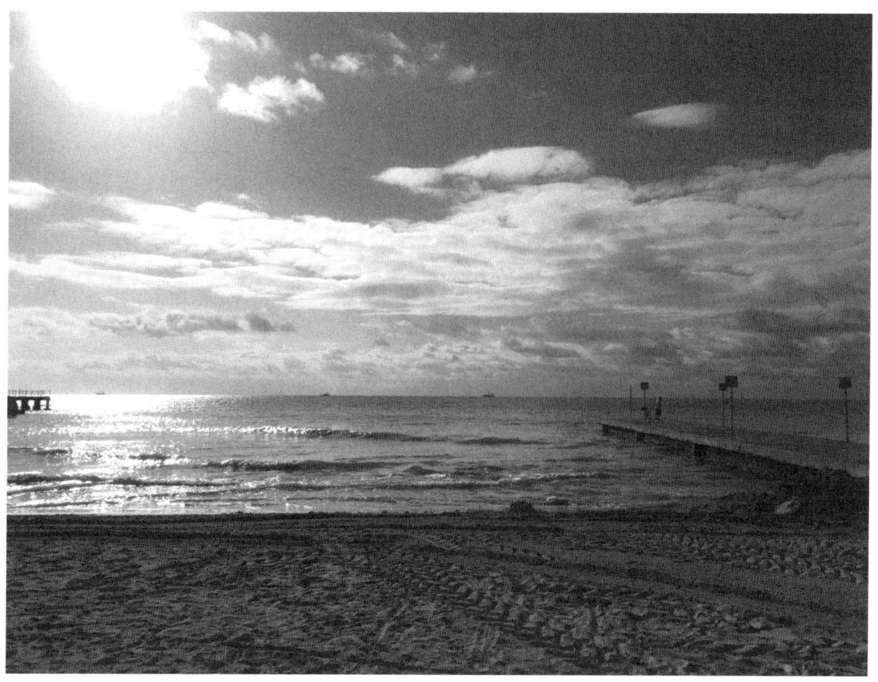

South Beach at the southern end of the island, perhaps where Hawkins and McRea stood that morning on February 9, 1829. *Photograph by Laura Albritton.*

each man fired a total of four shots apiece. William Whitehead recorded that "Hawkins' first ball passed through McRea's overcoat and glanced—his second went through his pantaloons, near the waistband, bruising his body—the third passed through his hat, and the fourth lodged in his thigh near the body and terminated the contest." The attorney's aim did not prove as true: "Only one short [*sic*] of McRea's touched his adversary, the third, which slightly grazed Hawkins' wrist."[12]

With that, the duel ended. Dr. Lacy would have rushed to tend to McRea's wounds, most especially the ball that entered his thigh—where blood soon soaked his trouser leg. Although potentially a fatal injury, the young man's luck held. After presumably applying a tourniquet around his friend's leg, the doctor would have surmised that the duelist might live. Hawkins, who had merely been grazed, would have wrapped his wrist in a handkerchief and left the beach triumphant. His honor had been salvaged, the insult to his marriage avenged. Although the gunfight had taken place on the very fringes of the Florida territory, at every stage, the proper decorum for dueling had been observed.

The tradition of dueling in western society stretches back centuries, with roots in the Middle Ages, when knights fought in hand-to-hand combat for reasons of honor. Later in seventeenth- and eighteenth-century Europe, the practice of dueling once again became popular, particularly among the aristocracy. One might say that the upper classes made a fetish, almost a cult, of personal honor. A man might challenge another to a duel to avenge some insult or offense, even for matters that to our modern sensibilities seem trivial. Men fought with swords until, in the nineteenth century, dueling with pistols became more the norm. Often the combatants did not duel "to the death," but rather to the drawing of first blood. Even so, a duel did entail risking one's life to assuage wounded, generally masculine pride. (Duels between women, although rare, did occur.)

In the United States, even the most educated, accomplished of men resorted to the severe justice of the duel, as evidenced by the tragic confrontation in 1804 between Vice President Aaron Burr and former secretary of the treasury Alexander Hamilton. Andrew Jackson, who was elected president of the United States in 1828, had fought several and possibly dozens of duels, including one in which he killed a man. The Carolina native, war hero and onetime military governor of Florida[13] would hastily respond to a perceived slander or slight by demanding satisfaction. Andrew Jackson once counseled a friend on dueling strategy: "The first rule is to let each man, fire when he pleases—so that he fires one minute or two after the word—Charge your friend to preserve his fire—to keep *his teeth firmly* clenched and *his fingers* in a position that if fired on and *hit*, his fire may not be extorted—sometimes when the distance is long it is agreed that both or either, may advance and fire."[14] While dueling gradually fell out of favor in the North as the nineteenth century progressed, in the South, particularly among the aristocratic planter class, the dangerous practice persisted for longer: "Duels, after all, were fought in defense of what the law could not defend—a gentleman's sense of personal honor—and nowhere were gentlemen more exquisitely sensitive on that point than in the future Confederacy."[15]

After his duel with McRea, Hawkins very likely would have considered the matter closed, since he had bested his opponent and inflicted real injury. As for his errant wife, one account records that immediately after discovering her with the seductive attorney, and even before the duel took place, Captain Hawkins had bundled her onto a ship in Key West's harbor and sent her away.[16] Now publicly avenged, the captain set sail for Mexico, where he had been serving in that young country's navy. This was in February; Key West's small community would not see the hotheaded captain again until May.

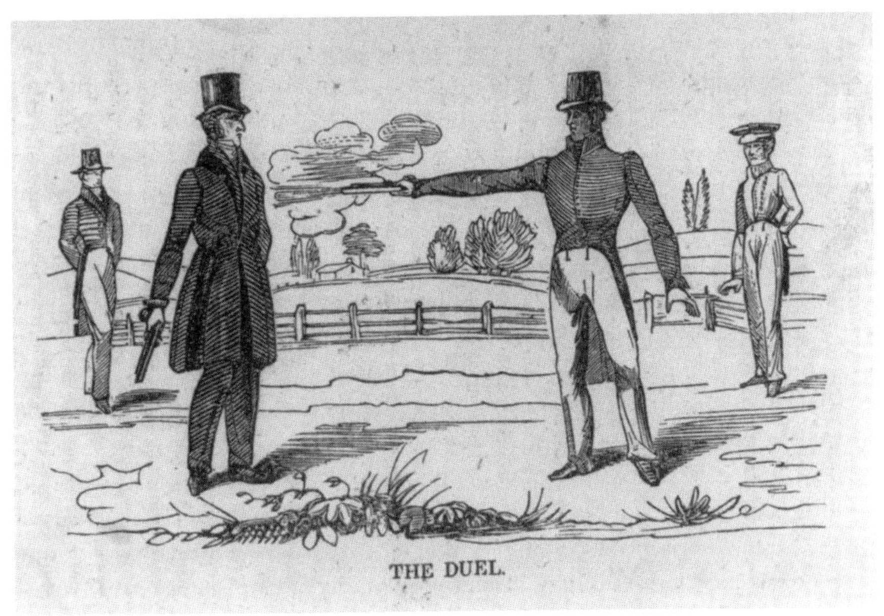

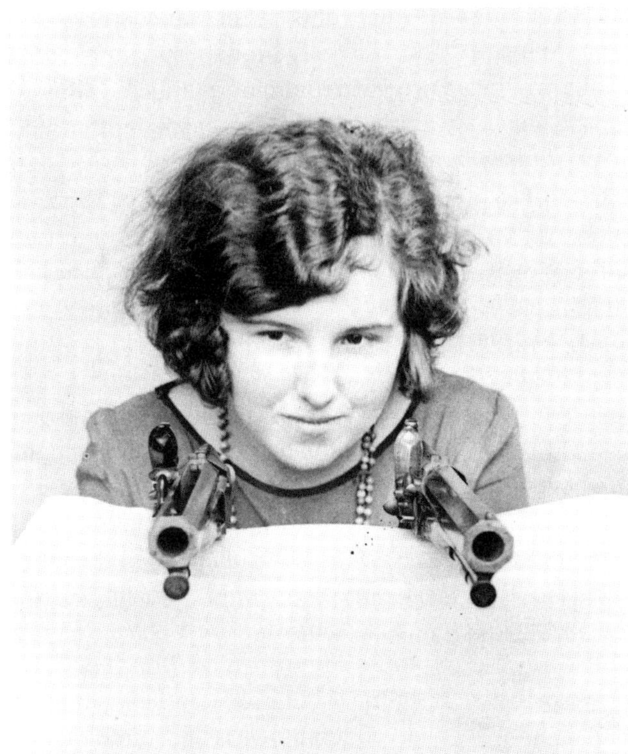

Above: An illustration of Andrew Jackson engaged in a duel. *Courtesy of the Library of Congress.*

Left: A young woman poses with Andrew Jackson's dueling pistols. Hawkins and McRea would have used very similar weapons. *Courtesy of the Library of Congress.*

In the meantime, attorney William Allison McRea slowly healed from his gunshot wounds. Although the initial danger of dying from loss of blood had been avoided, infection to the thigh wound posed a serious threat. The medical profession at that time had little understanding of how infection occurred or the importance of hygiene. Yet McRea turned out to be an exceptionally fortunate man, having survived not only one previous duel (with Algernon Thruston) but now two. Before long, townspeople spotted him hobbling along with a pair of crutches.[17] After Captain Hawkins departed, the five hundred or so residents of the island could not fail to note that another actor in the drama—Mrs. Hawkins herself—had returned to Key West. A duel had occurred, yes, but the saga of this romantic triangle was far from over.

We know little about the woman who inspired the two men to draw pistols against each other that February morning on the beach. Decades after the event, Key West pioneer William Whitehead recorded that this naïve young lady possessed "some literary attainments and personal attractions." Mrs. Hawkins, allegedly the captain's second wife, perhaps wrote poetry and likely had pleasant features and a nice figure. Married to a vain man who enjoyed showing off his military uniform, Mrs. Hawkins probably maintained a collection of handsome dresses; in a town where men outnumbered women by a very large margin, she would have attracted considerable male attention. On the other hand, she would have found little to no female companionship there. Key West in 1829—with its isolation and scattering of homes, wharves and warehouses—must have been a challenging place to live for a young woman with "literary attainments." We can surmise how she felt about her marriage to the captain by what occurred next.

With her husband away for months, Mrs. Hawkins once again became involved with the young attorney from Virginia. How intimately did they become involved? No one recorded those details, but it would be a mistake to assume that the young couple merely read each other sonnets by candlelight. At this point, the record tells us that "McRea was again in full use of his limb, and in the enjoyment of perfect health."[18] With its tiny population and limited geography, the island of Key West was one of the worst possible places to keep an affair secret. Why the two young people took such a risk, knowing Charles Hawkins's reaction that past February, one will never know. Perhaps McRea was simply a rake or the unsophisticated Mrs. Hawkins easily swayed. Perhaps their attraction for each other proved irresistible or they had genuinely fallen in love. In that era, upper-class and middle-class women often had little control over their own lives or destinies; it was not

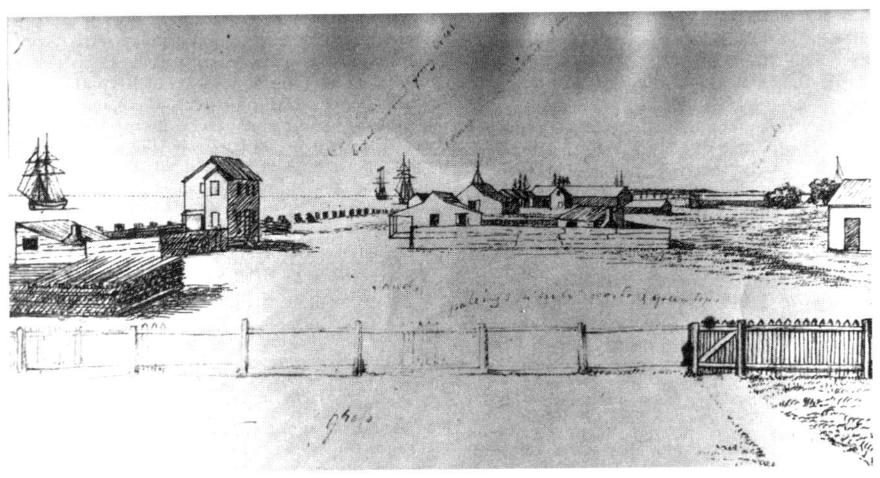

A drawing of Key West completed by Titian Peale in 1826 highlights how small the community was. *Courtesy of the Monroe County Public Library, Key West.*

uncommon for teenage girls to be pushed into matrimony with much older husbands as a way of lightening their families' financial burdens. Young Mrs. Hawkins may well have felt a prisoner in her own marriage.

According to a newspaper account published in June, Charles Hawkins "had been absent for four months, when on his return, he learned that his wife had been sent to her family by the friends of Capt. H. on account of the renewal of her intercourse with M'Crea, and that Mr. M'Crea had stated publicly this improper conduct to Mrs. H."[19]

As if the renewal of the affair wasn't enough, the young lawyer also betrayed his former client's business interests. "M'Crea had further aggravated Hawkins," a Virginia newspaper reported, "by receiving a fee and appearing as counsel for the opponents of Hawkins, on the pending law suits, after having been *feed* [paid a fee] by Hawkins, and in possession of all the facts necessary in behalf of Hawkins."[20] In other words, the lawyer McRea "was now using his knowledge of [his former client's] business affairs in *representing clients* suing Hawkins."[21]

If February's events had infuriated the captain, these latest developments must have left him in a blind rage. William McRea, ever the optimist, seems to have dismissed any concerns over his safety, as he neither hid nor left town. On this occasion, however, Captain Hawkins had no intention of submitting to the requirements of a duel. William Whitehead recorded that "on Sunday morning, May 24th, as McRea was walking up Whitehead Street, he received in his back from a double-barreled gun in the hands of Hawkins, who was secreted in a house on the South side of Whitehead Street, no less than thirty-three shot, and in two hours was a corpse." Suddenly, the daring Virginian lawyer was dead. By the next day, he was buried in Key West soil.[22]

After shooting McRea, Captain Hawkins turned himself in to the authorities. The marshal at Key West feared for his prisoner's safety and took him by ship to a more secure jail at St. Augustine.[23] After he arrived in the northern city on Florida's east coast, Hawkins awaited trial for murder. The case appeared clear cut: a duel was one thing, shooting a man in the back another. No challenge had been issued, no duel site agreed on, no seconds chosen—a man had simply been waylaid and executed. Yet this surprising tale does not end with Captain Hawkins been led to the gallows and hanged.

Key West chronicler William Whitehead claimed that the captain, apparently now divorced from his faithless wife, wooed and wed another young woman while imprisoned in St. Augustine. How the captain managed this feat while incarcerated on charges of murder remains a mystery. When he was finally returned to Key West, "no prison worthy of his acceptance as a place of residence" could be located, and "as to finding a qualified and unbiased Jury, that was therefore an impossibility."[24] As a result, Captain Hawkins, although technically still a prisoner, was free to enjoy life in Key West as he did before the crime.

For months, the national press reported on the developments of the scandal. In October 1830, Florida's territorial governor, William Duval, addressed the Legislative Council and spoke of McRea's murder by Hawkins. The governor "used the 'Key West Tragedy' to argue for tougher sanctions against dueling."[25] Captain Hawkins's actions had become a cause célèbre.

Nothing further progressed with the case for some time. At last, more than a year and a half after Hawkins was taken prisoner, Florida's Legislative Council stepped in. (It may have helped that at the time, Monroe County's representative, Richard Fitzpatrick, was an enthusiastic supporter of dueling.[26]) In January 1831, "An Act for the Relief of Charles E. Hawkins" was passed. The act stated as justification that "by the shewing of the said petitions, he can never be tried in the said district, because the citizens when summoned as jurymen, in the said case, generally answer on oath, that they believe the said Charles E. Hawkins ought to be acquitted."[27]

All of Monroe County's qualified jurors, free white men, believed Hawkins to be innocent of murder. As far as they were concerned, the captain had merely defended his honor. The act further mentioned "the great expense of his confinement, already amounting to the sum of near sixteen hundred dollars" and that "his continuance in custody...would in all probability amount to perpetual imprisonment, in violation of the liberty of the citizen."[28] No concern was shown for the rights of the dead man, shot in the back as he ventured out on a late spring morning. The implication was that McRea got what he deserved. As for the unfortunate young woman who fell for McRea's charms, "Mrs. H," she would disappear into the thickets of history. How she felt about her lover's death, or her ex-husband's release from all charges, is not written down, at least not in any records we have found. If she loved William McRea, the outcome of the case would have been particularly devastating. Divorced and publicly outed as an adulterer, she may have lived out her remaining years as a social pariah.

On January 28, 1831, Captain Charles E. Hawkins became a free man. He would move to Texas, where he achieved the rank of commodore in the Texas Navy. He served there with distinction. In 1837, after putting in his ship at the port of New Orleans, he contracted smallpox in that city and died. He was only thirty-five.[29] The following year, in yet another remarkable twist, Florida's Legislative Council struck down a law that had been passed to prevent duels. For the time being, dueling in Florida was no longer a crime.[30]

CHAPTER 2

THE RISE AND FALL OF RICHARD FITZPATRICK

In 1822, when Richard Fitzpatrick first disembarked from the sloop that had carried him to Key West, he would have seen a town still in the midst of being born. A few tall-masted ships rocked next to a wharf, where men were unloading cargo under the midday sun. Beyond the industry of the seafront, the thirty-year-old Fitzpatrick, squinting in the bright light, would have been able to make out wood-frame warehouses and a few simple homes. Navy officers in smart blue trousers and jackets strode by. Most of the citizens of this young outpost went on foot, walking along a dirt path, although occasionally, the *clip-clop* of a horse could be heard. It was hardly an impressive sight, especially to a wealthy planter from South Carolina.

Fitzpatrick would have set sail from Charleston, a city founded in 1670 and known for its fine architecture and gracious manners; by comparison, Key West appeared laughably rustic, even crude. But this would not have bothered Richard Fitzpatrick in the least. On the contrary, it must have filled him with optimism. Here was a place where he could make an impression. Here was a town where no one, with the possible exception of the enslaved men and women who had accompanied him on his voyage, knew of the family scandals he had fled back in South Carolina.

Richard Fitzpatrick bore an ancient Irish surname, with the family motto "the strong will yield to the strong," a philosophy that perfectly summed up the young man's attitude toward the world. Wealthy, intelligent and determined to create his own sphere of influence, the young Carolina planter wasted no time in establishing himself in Key West. Money and self-

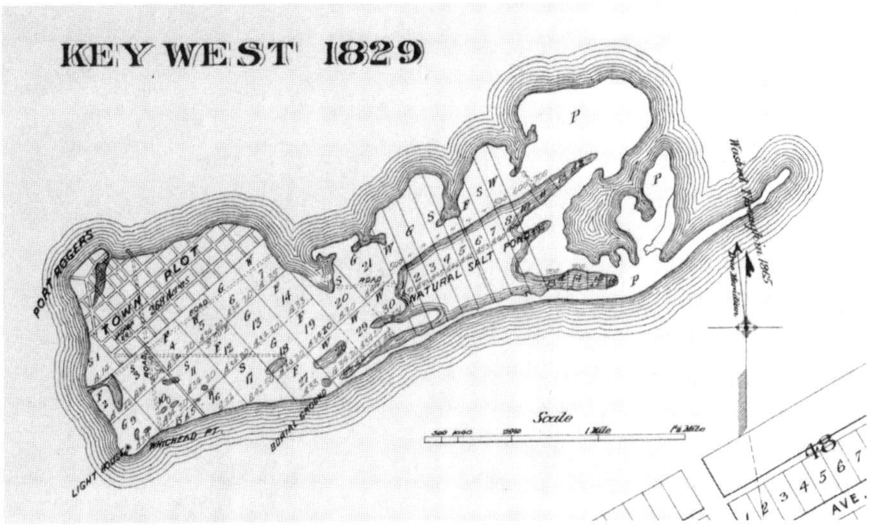

A map of Key West from 1829, seven years after Richard Fitzpatrick arrived on the island. *Courtesy of the Monroe County Public Library, Key West.*

confidence could carry someone a long way on this rough-and-tumble island frontier. Fitzpatrick arrived a mere year after Florida was officially ceded by Spain to the United States—the same year the island's owner, Juan Pablo Salas, sold his property to Americans. He had also arrived just as wrecking was about to become Key West's major industry.

On the southern side of the Florida Keys stretches an intricate underwater thicket of corals, which, in that era, made the waters very difficult to navigate. Ships from Havana, Cartagena and other ports regularly foundered on the treacherous Florida Reef. It became clear that a man could earn a fortune in wrecking, or salvaging these many vessels. Using Key West as their base, wreckers began to rescue valuable cargo and, when possible, the crew; in return, they received a percentage of the profits from the cargo's sale. Richard Fitzpatrick inserted himself into this youthful industry by establishing himself as the acting deputy auctioneer—in fact, the only *resident* auctioneer—for all the wrecking cargo brought into Key West. At a time when wrecking was still largely unregulated, the position of auctioneer gave Fitzpatrick considerable power. Standing in front of an eagerly bidding crowd, the southern aristocrat would have had no hesitation in asserting himself. To profit even more, Fitzpatrick purchased his own wrecking sloop, the *Eagle*, in the mid-1820s.[31]

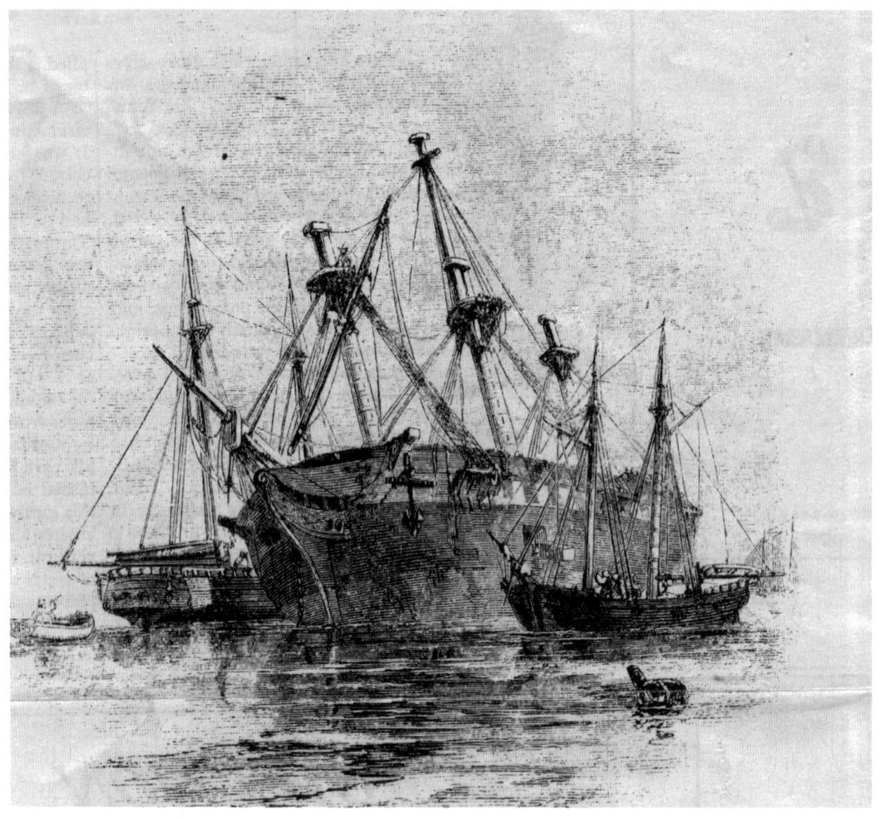

Wreckers rescuing cargo from a ship that foundered on the Florida Reef. *Courtesy of the Monroe County Public Library, Key West.*

Showing a natural ambition, the thirty-year-old managed to get himself appointed to a succession of government positions, including wrecking property appraiser, judge of election results, grand jury foreman, town councilman, notary public and, when the U.S. Navy abandoned Key West for Pensacola, guardian of the remaining naval property.[32] By 1827, a mere five years after his arrival in Key West, Richard Fitzpatrick had achieved an impressive new height, becoming the clerk of the newly established Monroe County Court. Two years later, when a young William Whitehead mapped out the streets of Key West, he named one of them Fitzpatrick Street.[33]

We may not know how Fitzpatrick looked physically (although with his Irish background, it is possible he had light eyes and pale skin), but his temperament and character are another story. Fitzpatrick hailed from South Carolina's planter caste, which had fashioned itself into kind of

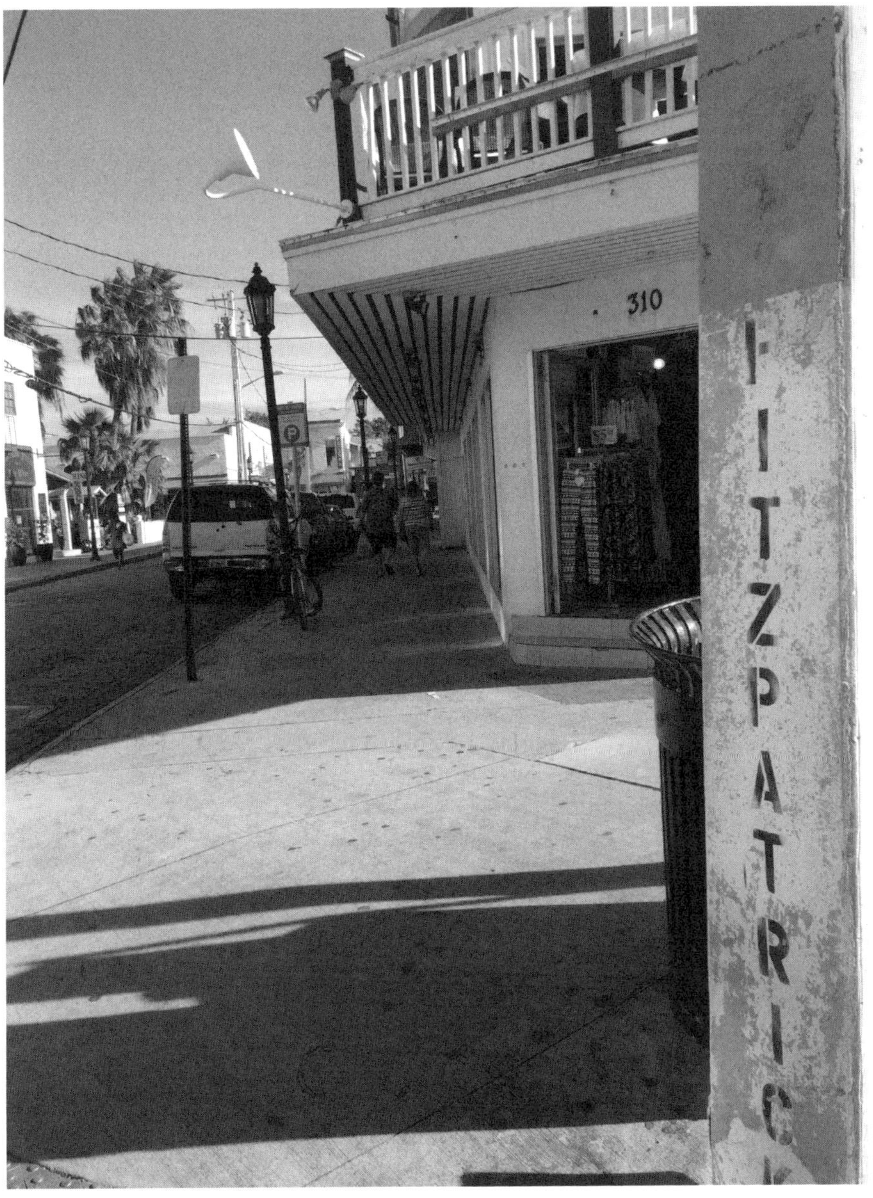

Fitzpatrick Street, which runs between Greene and Front Streets, as it appears today. *Photograph by Laura Albritton.*

quasi-aristocracy, a system based on the ownership of massive tracts of land and built on slave labor, with its own elaborate social mores and codes of honor. (Richard Fitzpatrick not only believed in dueling in matters of honor, but he also thought any man who did not accept a challenge was a no-account coward.)[34]

Initially, the few hundred townspeople of Key West seemed willing to defer to the rich, opinionated plantation owner. Well educated, well spoken and in all likelihood elegantly dressed, Richard Fitzpatrick possessed polish, one quality that was in short supply. Key West's small population consisted mainly of sea captains, sailors and merchants, with a few professional men, and Fitzpatrick, as a man of significant property, stood apart. After all, his father, William Fitzpatrick, had served as an officer in America's Revolutionary War and, later, as a member of South Carolina's General Assembly, and he had owned a cotton plantation, Bell Hall, of ten thousand acres.[35] While townspeople may have grown a bit weary of Fitzpatrick's accounts of his illustrious background and his mansion back in the vicinity of Columbia, what they did not realize was that, in reality, the Fitzpatrick family were social outcasts.

Shortly after Richard was born, his father, William, abandoned his wife, Richard's mother, and took up with a young woman named Elizabeth Gillespie. The scandal only increased when Elizabeth gave birth to William's illegitimate son. To further compound the situation, William later attempted to partially disinherit his legitimate children, Richard and Harriet, in favor of his mistress and their child. Knowing that William had rejected his first and legitimate family for this new one must have been traumatic to the young Richard. When the old man finally died after suffering from dementia, the battle over his estate waged in the courts for years.[36] In the end, Richard Fitzpatrick inherited the bulk of the property and sixty slaves, but wealth could not erase the social stigma. Richard's mother; his sister, Harriet; and Richard himself were all tainted by association; they may not have been "received" in polite society. When he left South Carolina behind, Richard Fitzpatrick may have been distancing himself from the painful memories of his father's abandonment and the disgrace William visited on the family name. One might also speculate that his father's rejection left Richard Fitzpatrick with a desperate need to prove himself.

One of the first intimations that Fitzpatrick could be a difficult character was a series of disputes with another of Key West's early settlers, Pardon C. Greene. Their disagreements over money and a wharf led to lawsuits and countersuits; the two men became enemies.[37] Unfortunately, alienating people emerged as something of a habit with Richard Fitzpatrick. Always on the lookout for a way to increase his wealth, Fitzpatrick leased property from William Whitehead in order to start a salt-making business. As a slave owner, he had the labor source for this hot, tedious activity and could see its potential, since salt was a valuable commodity. Key Westers paid close attention, for if the island were to become a leader in salt-making, it would mean increased shipping and thus new prosperity for the port. Not content merely to develop a saltworks, he also decided to run for a seat on Florida's Legislative Council as the representative of Monroe County. Fitzpatrick won that election by twenty-one votes; his only rival was one George Weaver of Indian Key. The tiny, eleven-acre island of Indian Key (in today's Islamorada) was home to wreckers and would gradually become a wrecking headquarters to rival Key West; most Indian Key residents voted for Weaver, while most Key Westers voted for Fitzpatrick.[38]

Having won elected office, Richard Fitzpatrick might have consolidated his popularity by encouraging Key West's nascent salt-making industry. Instead, he did the opposite. When the "Act to Incorporate the North American Salt Company" at Key West was brought before Florida's Legislative Council, rather than promote its passage, Richard Fitzpatrick maneuvered to defeat it. In fact, the act never even came to a vote. Why oppose something so obviously in Key West's interest? Fitzpatrick's opposition probably had something to do with Pardon Greene's support for it, but additionally, he did not want any competition for his own saltworks.[39]

His opposition to the saltworks did not endear him to Key West voters. Yet another action alienated voters even further, when he supported "An Act to Incorporate the City of Key West," which, on the face of it, sounded innocuous. However, the act would have allowed the mayor and aldermen to "levy a tax on improved and real estate within said city."[40] Needless to say, the prospect of new taxes infuriated men of property, including Pardon Greene. Because Fitzpatrick himself owned little or no land in Key West, the act would have caused him no serious inconvenience or loss of income. While he may have possessed charm and beautiful manners, it was also emerging that the South Carolinian had a tin ear, politically speaking.

This time, Richard Fitzpatrick paid a price for flouting the wishes of his constituency and lost the next election. To compound the bitterness of the loss, the man who won his seat on the Legislative Council was Ed Chandler, attorney for his nemesis, Pardon Greene.[41] Such a defeat might have humbled another man, perhaps even taught him a lesson in political realities, but not Richard Fitzpatrick. His pride seems to have blinded him.

In 1829, an advertisement for land appeared in the pages of the *Key West Register* newspaper that gave Fitzpatrick a new cause for hope. The Florida Keys, while extraordinarily beautiful islands, had relatively little land to cultivate, but James Egan and others were offering to sell vast acreage farther north, at New River (or present-day Fort Lauderdale) and at the mouth of the Miami River, just north of the Seminoles' Little Hunting Grounds. With characteristic enthusiasm for a new venture, Richard Fitzpatrick purchased multiple parcels for a total of 2,660 acres.[42] Surveying this virgin territory, with its thick tangle of subtropical forest, he could imagine a neat and orderly plantation, with a grand manor house perhaps built from coral rock and fields manned by his own African slaves. Here he could establish a new planter society, far from the gossips of South Carolina. Fitzpatrick hired an overseer and had crops sown in a place where no planter had previously dared invest, given its obscure location and the proximity of Indians. The next year, in 1830, fields of sugarcane, their green fringed tops tossing in the breeze, stretched clear to the horizon. Already Fitzpatrick could boast of one hundred cultivated acres.[43] The land at New River he leased to a farmer and slaveholder named William Cooley. Now, he had vested interests across Monroe County, from Key West to the Miami River[44] and beyond.

Fifty to sixty black men, owned by Fitzpatrick, labored each day while Fitzpatrick attended to his interests in the Keys. One Key West resident, Stephen Mallory, came to stay on the plantation in 1831. Mallory admired Fitzpatrick's attempt to bring southern plantation culture to South Florida and later recounted that "all the fruits of the tropics grow, or will grow without replanting" and that it was "worked by some fifty or sixty servants."[45] (Mallory heartily approved of slavery. As a U.S. senator, he would later make an impassioned speech defending the South's peculiar institution.) Both in his Key West salt-making operation and on his Miami River property, slavery remained, at least in Richard Fitzgerald's mind, essential to his success.

The lawyer William Hackley recorded in his diary on May 7, 1831, that "Richard Fitzpatrick arrived [at Key West] from Charleston with some 28 to 30 Negroes in the Schooner *Venus*."[46] Charleston, South Carolina, possessed one of the largest slave markets in the South, a place where men, women and children were inspected, bought and sold like plow horses. Whether the slaves he transported to Key West were men and women he had purchased in Charleston or slaves his family already owned is not known. In Fitzpatrick's world view, owning human beings was not only an economic necessity but also the natural order of things. When slave revolts occurred, such as Nat Turner's Rebellion in August 1831, it only hardened the resolve of southern planters like Fitzpatrick to keep African Americans, both enslaved and free, under the heel of whites.

After losing the election to Florida's Legislative Council, Richard Fitzpatrick took up a new cause as Key West justice of the peace: the enforcement of an act that made it illegal for "any free negro or mulatto to migrate, or be brought into this Territory." This act was designed to keep free men and women of color from migrating to Florida; the fear among whites, particularly slave owners like Fitzpatrick, was that additional numbers of free African Americans would aid their enslaved brothers and sisters in a revolt. Fitzpatrick pursued enforcement of this law in an extreme fashion and went after free Key West blacks who had made brief trips out of Florida, claiming that upon their return (to their own homes) they were "migrating" into the territory. In his single-minded pursuit to rid the island of as many free blacks as possible, Fitzgerald eventually tangled with Key West lawyer William Hackley in a court case.[47] Hackley disapproved of Fitzpatrick's position, noting that his refusal to grant an appeal was "illegal and unjust."[48] It wasn't the first time Hackley and Fitzpatrick would clash nor the first time that Fitzpatrick would demonstrate vindictiveness toward people of color.

Fitzpatrick took his revenge on Ed Chandler—and his client, Pardon Greene—by winning the next election. Once again, he served as Monroe County's representative to Florida's Legislative Council, in 1835. Yet apparently, he had learned nothing from his prior defeat: in 1835, Fitzpatrick moved to repeal the 1832 Act for Incorporating Key West. The subsequent bill he developed would have directed "the City Council to turn over all the tax money in the City Council's possession to the Justices of the Peace in the city."[49] Fitzpatrick believed that justices of the peace, or JPs, would be better qualified than the city council to administer Key West's tax revenue. It hardly escaped Key Westers' notice that Fitzpatrick was a justice of the peace himself. The move was breathtaking in its gall and self-interest. The local newspaper protested that the "bill professes also to give power to any Justice of the Peace, disposed to act the petty tyrant, to take the private individual's property of the members of this board for public uses."[50] Once again, Richard Fitzpatrick infuriated his own constituency. As a result of this latest tone-deaf maneuver, he came close to losing the 1836 election to William Hackley; his margin of victory in Key West was a meager three votes.[51] Instead of agonizing over how he might regain the esteem of the local voters, however, he would discover a strategy to ensure a triumph without having to win a single Key West supporter.

While Fitzpatrick schemed to advance his career, the Second Seminole War broke out in Florida. The Seminoles, a tribe of Creek Indians who had fled persecution farther north, arrived in Florida in the eighteenth century and later allied themselves with escaped slaves. Once Spain ceded Florida to the United States, American settlers pressured the U.S. government to get rid of these native peoples who also needed land to survive. The second war erupted as Seminoles attempted to avoid removal from Florida, which pushed the remaining resistors deeper and deeper south, into the Miami region and the Everglades, into the region where Richard Fitzpatrick's dream of a glorious plantation had taken root.

Alarmed by the threat to his property, Fitzpatrick volunteered for duty. He arrived at the army camp in high style, with his own horses and a slave to wait on him. He served as aide-de-camp to General Clinch and then later General Call. In this environment, his charisma made a favorable impression. "Rich, generous, and patriotic" were words used to describe the dashing, confident politician.[52] Soon, he rose to the rank of colonel. He hoped that going to war, just as his father had done in the American Revolution, would safeguard his property from the Indians.

Colonel Fitzpatrick's military service ended in 1836, a year that initially seemed lucky for the man. In 1836, his fellow representatives in Tallahassee gathered together and voted to elect the Monroe County man as the president of the Legislative Council. Now "Fizzy," as he was nicknamed in one newspaper, had genuine power as a respected and admired man of wealth and position. However, another event would change his fortunes once again. In 1836, a band of Indians attacked William Cooley's farm (on Fitzpatrick's land) at New River and killed his family.[53] Settlers all along the southeastern Florida coast evacuated to Indian Key or Key West, including everyone at Fitzpatrick's Miami River plantation. His overseer reported that his own slaves had resisted leaving, presumably because they hoped to flee and join up with the Indians.[54]

Over the next year, Fitzpatrick publicized his Miami River property in the hope that other people would buy land from him and settle there. But no one expressed interest: white settlers remained at Indian Key, Key Vacas in the Middle Keys and Key West. The army erected a camp, first on Key Biscayne and then on Richard Fitzpatrick's land. Named Fort Dallas, it would serve as an outpost against the Seminole Indians.

With the army occupying his land, his plantation fell into disrepair; fields lay fallow and untended. As if the ruin of his property weren't enough, Fitzgerald's hold on political power in Monroe County was under threat.

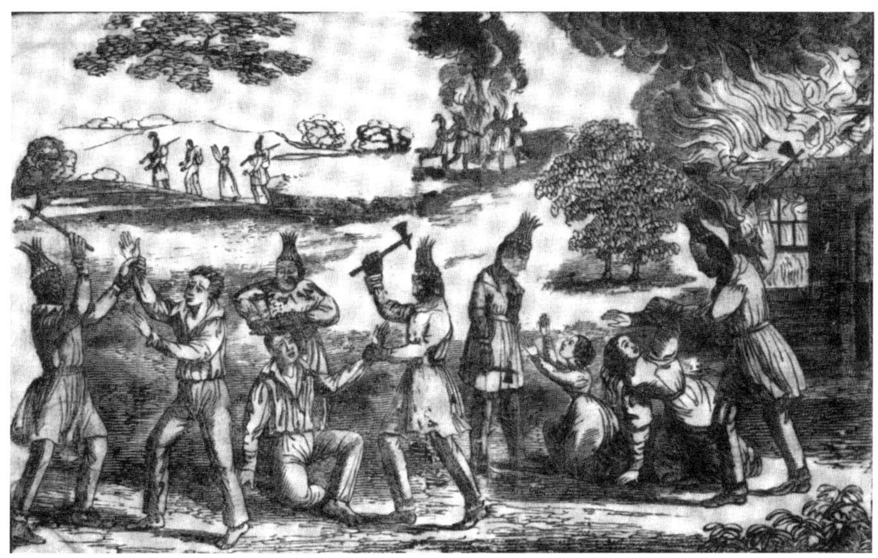

An illustration of white settlers being attacked by Seminole Indians in Florida. *Courtesy of the Library of Congress.*

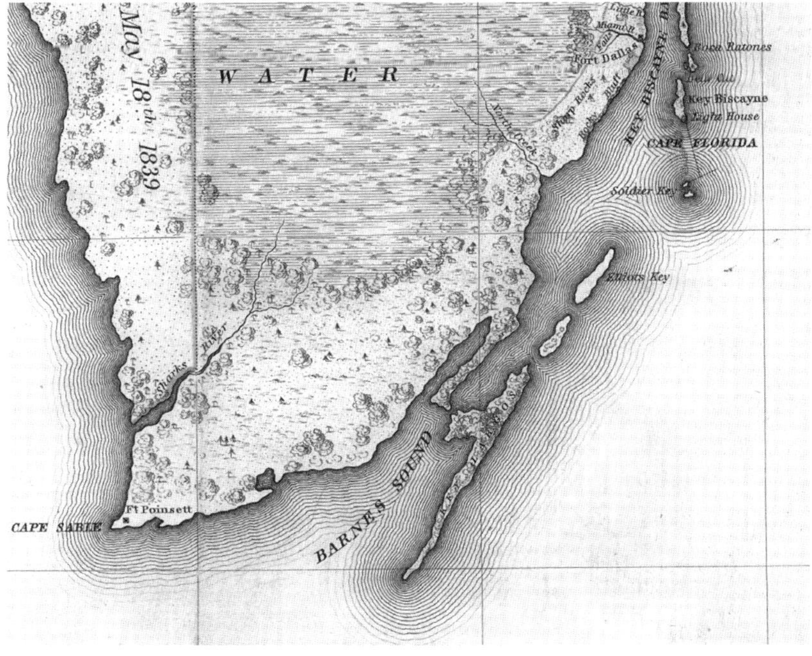

A detail from this 1839 map shows Fort Dallas at the Miami River. The Keys are omitted except for Key Largo. *Courtesy of the Library of Congress.*

The merchants, wreckers, sea captains and professionals of Key West, many hailing from New England or the Bahamas, once again felt stymied by their own representative. As a landowner and southern planter, Richard Fitzpatrick continued to take positions diametrically opposed to the interests of many Key Westers. He simply could not relate to them and their needs. William Hackley had almost defeated him for office in 1836; Fitzpatrick realized that if the situation continued, he would be out of office and stripped of power by 1837.

Now, casting his eye around the Florida Keys, his attention alighted on one John Jacob Housman, the "wrecker king of Indian Key."[55] For "several years," Fitzpatrick's nephew, William English, owned a house on this eleven-acre island.[56] The island served as a frequent stopping point for ships that sailed along the Florida Reef; it boasted warehouses, a hotel and streets, all presided over by Housman. Like Richard Fitzpatrick, Housman owned slaves and had built part of his fortune with slave labor. He had also been tarred by scandal. As a young man, Housman allegedly sailed from Staten Island down the Atlantic seaboard with one of his father's ships, the *William Henry*, essentially stealing a valuable asset from his own family.[57] In the Florida Keys, Housman engaged in wrecking from the 1820s, while he gained a reputation as someone who skirted and occasionally far overstepped the law. (The southern gentleman and the northern sea captain must have known each other in Key West in the 1820s, given the fact that Fitzpatrick served as a wrecking auctioneer.) Also like Fitzpatrick, Housman came into conflict with Key Westers. Indeed, it was Housman's clash with Key West's wrecking establishment that drove him to set up his own operation on Indian Key. Despite having another base of operations, John Jacob Housman still had to use Key West as a port of entry and frequently sparred with its admiralty court and customs officials.

One final commonality propelled these two unlikely allies together: the threat to their property from tribal peoples. Seminole Indians, driven deep into the Everglades and now the Florida Keys, had grown desperate to make a last stand against American incursion. Housman knew that Indian Key, small and remote as it was, had little defense against an attacking band of braves. Fitzpatrick and Housman believed that should the Indian threat not be "dealt with," their respective properties and dreams would be doomed. As far as Fitzpatrick and Housman were concerned, they faced two main foes: the Seminole Indians and the Key West establishment.

Soon John Jacob Housman hatched a scheme to get himself and Indian Key out from under the control of Key West: they would draw a new county

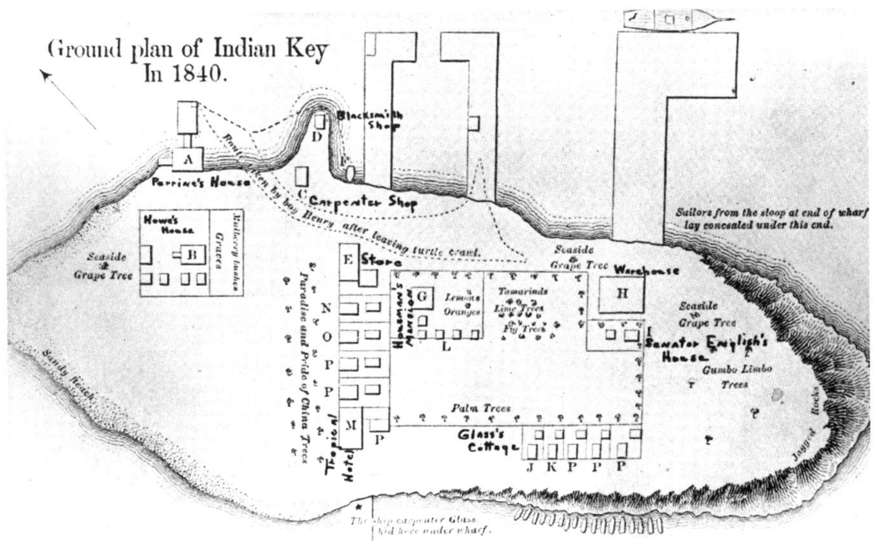

A drawing of Indian Key that includes the house of William English, Fitzpatrick's nephew. *Courtesy of the Monroe County Public Library, Key West.*

line right through the middle of the Florida Keys. Then Key West would not be able to interfere with Housman's wrecking interests on Indian Key. Housman may have despised Key West, but the antipathy was mutual. Attorney William Hackley felt such loathing of Housman's mini empire that he wrote in his diary during one 1832 voyage: "[R]emained on board all evening as I dislike Indian Key so much that unless I have business I am determined not to go to shore."[58]

If Richard Fitzpatrick had felt similar distaste toward Housman, then Housman's next maneuver would have gotten exactly nowhere. Housman submitted a petition that a new county should be formed within the Florida Keys and Cape Florida (present-day Miami), breaking off from Monroe, with Indian Key as the new county seat. Fifty-six other Monroe County residents, primarily from Indian Key and Cape Florida, signed the petition, which was submitted to the Legislative Council.[59] Their rationale for such a dramatic schism was that given the spread-out geography of the islands, men called for jury duty had to undergo unreasonable hardship, sailing long distances, often in poor weather, and remain in Key West on a stipend that did not adequately cover their expenses. "Some of them" lived "two hundred and thirty miles from the court house," the petition claimed.[60]

Presiding over the disparate legislators in Tallahassee, Fitzpatrick, as the president of Florida's Legislative Council, wielded real power and influence. After all, Monroe County was his home county, and he could have had the petition dismissed immediately. Instead, Fitzpatrick rounded up support so that the new bill creating Pinckney County passed unanimously. Before it passed, however, he deleted one crucial passage: "That the counties of Monroe and Pinckey, shall comprise one Election district for a member of the Legislative Council heretofore elected from Monroe County, until further provision be made for the same by act of Congress."[61]

This was not at all what Fitzpatrick wanted: instead, each county, Monroe and Pinckney, would have its own election districts. Key West was now, electorally speaking, cut off from Indian Key. One final alteration happened: the name Pinckney was changed to Dade in honor of Major Dade, who had been killed by Indians not long before.[62] The governor signed the new bill on January 28, 1836, before settlers in Key West or Key Vacas had any notion of what had been brewing in Tallahassee.

A furious response swelled up among Key Westers and among the seagoing pioneers settled at Key Vacas in the Middle Keys. Everyone in Key West knew that Housman now had even more autonomy for his little island empire; meanwhile, Middle Keys residents like Temple Pent Sr. chafed at the idea of being yoked in a district largely controlled by a man whom they considered a villain. Fitzpatrick, on the other hand, had orchestrated the situation in his favor. Although Dade County may not have been his own plan, he had identified how its creation could save and even cement his own power. In the following election, Fitzpatrick stood as a candidate out of Dade County and Indian Key, not Monroe County and Key West. He could use as a justification the fact that he owned vast property (his plantation) in the new county, even if he didn't reside there, given that it was occupied by Fort Dallas and armed forces. Key Vacas men supported their own candidate, while most Indian Key residents voted for Fitzpatrick. In 1837, Fitzpatrick returned triumphantly to the small territorial capital of Tallahassee as the brand-new representative of the newly created Dade County.

At this moment of triumph, neither Fitzpatrick nor Housman could have known that in four years, their dreams would be consigned to the dust heap. But they did feel the threat, as ominous as the early blow from a hurricane, of the Indians watching and waiting. Due to the army's fort and ongoing hostilities with the Seminoles, Richard Fitzpatrick's plantation in Miami bore little fruit and reaped no crops, while the slaves had to be housed and fed in the Florida Keys. His overenthusiastic investment in South Florida land threatened to ruin him. Fitzpatrick volunteered to sail to Cuba to buy and bring back ferocious bloodhounds, like the kind that had been used in Jamaica to hunt escaped slaves during the Maroon War. The chilling goal was to hunt down and eliminate Indians. Indeed, in 1839, the voyage commenced, and with great difficulty, Fitzpatrick returned to Florida's shores with thirty-three bloodhounds and three handlers.[63] This development appeared in newspapers. Across the United States, protests erupted at the thought of using dogs to chase after—and presumably kill—Indian men, women and children. In the end, his plan achieved virtually nothing. Separately, John Jacob Housman submitted an offer to the government to personally slaughter and capture Indians. (Housman's offer was not accepted.)

More startling still is Richard Fitzpatrick's 1840 letter to the Florida Congressional delegate that "those wily savages remain in the undisturbed possession of the country and are almost daily in the habit of committing the most horrid murders."[64] He then suggested that for a sum of $2.5 million he would go after the Seminoles: "[T]he plan which your memorialist and those who will operate with him intend to pursue and adopt is to take to the woods like Indians, eat, drink, and sleep like Indians; use all the arts and strategems which Indians do, and to fight the Indian in his own way."[65] In other words, Fitzpatrick would hire men and lead them himself into the Florida wilds, including the Everglades, to root out the remaining Indians and extinguish them. He claimed that he could personally do what an entire army had not yet accomplished. His desperation, coupled with arrogance, had rendered him delusional.

One wonders whether the Indians got wind of Fitzpatrick's and Housman's respective genocidal plans. Or was it merely a coincidence that on August 7, 1840, Indian warriors brought their dugout canoes silently ashore Indian Key before dawn? Led by Chief Chekika, they crept up to the houses and attacked. Seven individuals met with their deaths, while others, including Captain and Mrs. Housman, managed to escape. Most of Indian Key was consumed by flames.

Housman's empire had been reduced to ashes; the true, sorry statement of his finances meant that the man had virtually nothing left but to work in Key West on a wrecking vessel as a sailor. That same year, he died, crushed between two ships. Fitzpatrick's toehold on power also evaporated: with Indian Key deserted, his base was no more. With no one left to vote for him, and his land ruined and in the middle of a war zone, Richard Fitzpatrick gave up on both Monroe and Dade Counties. In 1842, his sister, Harriet, agreed to loan him more than $20,000, while he mortgaged his slaves and his land; his nephew, William English, then bought his Miami and New River properties.[66] Fitzpatrick quit the Florida territory and headed for Brownsville, Texas. Later, he would fight in the Mexican-American War and even win appointments as a diplomat. But his success never seemed to last. Despite his many privileges, one suspects that Richard Fitzpatrick's grandiosity and pride, coupled with an extreme desire to vindicate the family name, worked to defeat him. At one point, he and William English even tried their luck in the California Gold Rush, but that venture also failed. The southern aristocrat and onetime toast of Key West would die unheralded and virtually broke, far from the fiefdom he once tried to establish.

Chapter 3

Confederate Conchs Enlist

One of the most dramatic—and better-known—exploits to occur in the Florida Keys during the Civil War period took place when, on January 13, 1861, shortly after midnight, an army captain named John Brannan slipped his troops from their barracks on the northeastern side of Key West.[67] "In the dead of night," one soldier later recalled, Brannan secretly marched the men "by a route avoiding the town" to Fort Zachary Taylor on Key West's western shore.[68] The troops brought with them as many weapons and as much ammunition as they could carry.[69] There Brannan met up with Captain Edward Hunt's meager forces, mostly engineers and Northern laborers who had agreed to help, and together the assembled men seized the still-as-yet-unfinished Fort Taylor and barricaded themselves inside. Brannan's own force may have consisted of only forty-four men (while the island's white population numbered more than two thousand),[70] yet stored inside the fort were seventy thousand gallons of fresh water and "food provisions enough to last four months."[71] From behind the safety of its walls, and separated from the island by a narrow spit of land, the fort's armaments could fire on any insurrection in town and defend against an incursion by sea. Key Westers awoke the next morning to a new reality: their town had fallen under the control of the U.S. Army. With this single action, Brannan ensured that America's southernmost city and a strategically important port in Confederate Florida remained firmly in possession of the North.

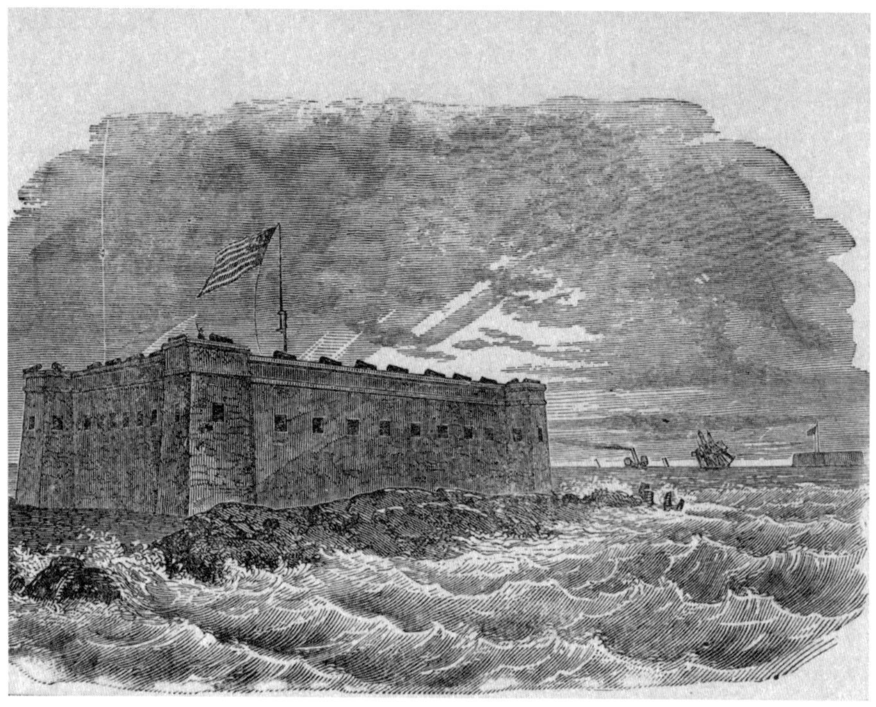

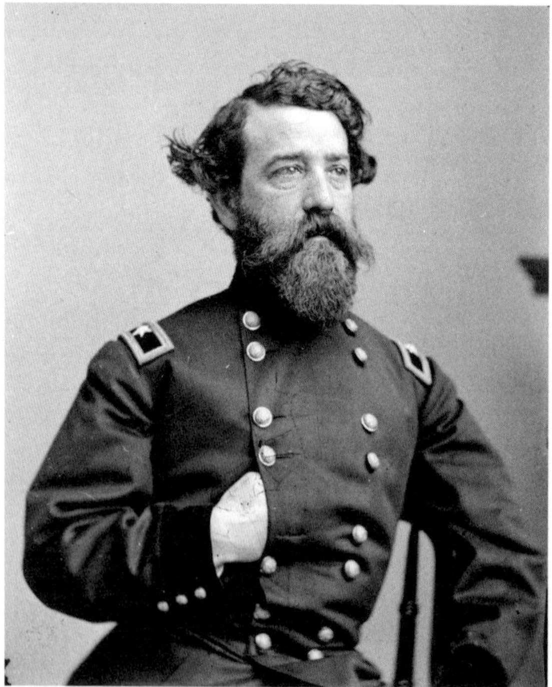

Above: Fort Zachary Taylor flying the Stars and Stripes. Construction was still ongoing here when Florida seceded from the Union. *Courtesy of the Library of Congress.*

Left: Army captain John Brannan acted decisively after news of Florida's secession reached Key West. *Courtesy of the Library of Congress.*

Captain Brannan, forty-two years old with exuberant waves of dark hair and a resplendent beard and mustache, had responded decisively to changing events. Ever since the election of Abraham Lincoln in November 1860 (when Lincoln won the electoral college but only 40 percent of the popular vote), Southern states had grown increasingly agitated; secession loomed not as a theoretical exercise but as a concrete possibility. Florida's governor picked January 3 for a convention to decide the state's future: remain with the Union or secede. In Key West, Monroe County's bigwigs, all white men, met to elect delegates; pro-Union man Walter Maloney Sr. was outnumbered by pro-secession voters, and the islands' delegates—Judge Winer Bethel, William Pinckney and Asa Tift—intended to vote for Florida to quit the United States.[72] On January 10, in the Tallahassee capitol, the Florida Keys representatives along with fifty-nine others voted for and then on January 11 signed the Ordinance of Secession.

In those days, news traveled to Key West by schooner and sloop, not television or Internet. It would have taken two days for Key Westers to learn the result of the state convention. As the convention's outcome reached the island, Captain Brannan quickly grasped the significance of the situation. The U.S. Army forces in the barracks and the men working to complete Fort Taylor were thick in the midst of enemy territory. Brannan, with Captain Hunt's encouragement, did not wait for approval from Washington. He took the initiative and, in about six hours, secured a highly strategic location for the U.S. government.

These events are well documented and certainly not "hidden," but this episode provides important context for what will follow later. Because we know that Union troops secured the island months before the Rebel attack on Fort Sumter, it was conceivable that Key West's citizens would embrace their new status as a Northern stronghold in a Southern state. Although some Southerners resided in the Keys, many residents hailed from the Bahamas, New England, Cuba and even Europe. Why would Yankees and foreigners support the South? It would be natural to assume that Key West and its multi-ethnic citizenry spent the duration of the Civil War as a cooperative, loyal Union outpost. But surprisingly, some Key Westers, along with settlers at Indian Key and Key Vacas, were not united behind the Union. In fact, it was in light of widespread Confederate sympathies that Brannan acted so swiftly, taking Fort Taylor and then reporting to his superior, "I have placed my entire command in Fort Taylor for the purpose of protecting it. I shall, until orders from the General Government to the contrary, defend it."[73] Later in February, the captain did not "apprehend

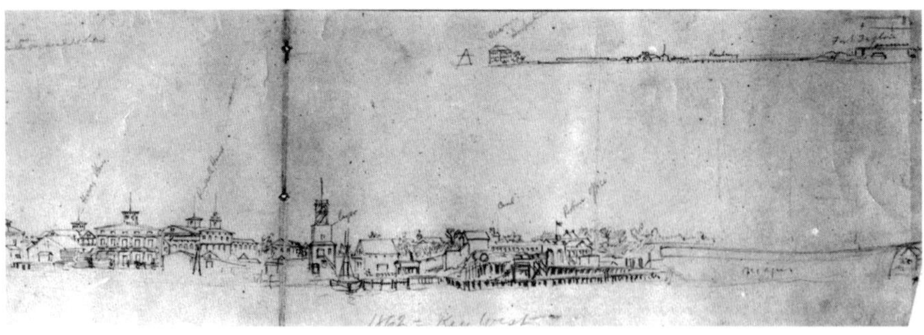

A sketch of the Key West waterfront during the Civil War. *Courtesy of the Monroe County Public Library, Key West.*

any attack on this fort," yet he observed pro-secession flags flying over several shops.[74]

The War Between the States, the War of Rebellion, the Civil War—call it what you will. The conflict that would erupt a few months later would find neighbor divided against neighbor and brothers enlisting to fight their own brothers. Key West was no exception. Fervent supporters of the Confederacy found themselves in opposition to Unionists whom they had known and befriended over decades, and at least in one case, the terrible war would pit a father against his own son.

One of the early troublemakers for occupying Union forces was Henry Mulrennan, a tall, good-looking military veteran originally from Scotland.[75] As a Key West shopkeeper, he embraced the South's cause with all the enthusiasm of the newly converted. About two months after the events at Fort Taylor, Mulrennan hoisted a secessionist flag (possibly the Bonnie Blue, blue with one white star) at his store. Unfurled against the clear March skies above his wood shingle roof, the flag fluttered like a provocation to the Union forces. In a letter to Captain Brannan,[76] Mulrennan wrote, "The flag of the Republic of Florida having been hoisted this day and properly saluted by military officers holding commissions under that republic, we consider you gentlemen enough to acknowledge it accordingly." He had the audacity to add, "P.S. You will treat the bearer [of this letter] with all the courtesy due to military men."[77] If Mulrennan expected his flag to be saluted by Brannan, he was in for a disappointment. His pro-Rebel agitating did not end there, however, and by June, with the war underway, the man was arrested (or possibly just threatened with arrest) and forced to leave Key West as a result of his "treasonable and seditious language."[78] Although Henry Mulrennan disappears from some Key West accounts at this point, he would reemerge later.

Mulrennan was not the only one unable to abide the Union occupation. Key Wester Robert Watson wrote in his diary in September 1861, "Owing to the political affairs of the country and the Federal troops having possession of this place and as it is rather unsafe for a southern man to live here I have determined to leave in disgust."[79] Twenty-six-year-old Robert worked as a carpenter, probably doing a good amount of work on ships; his family had moved from the Bahamas to Key West when he was an adolescent, and now this naturalized citizen prepared to take up arms on behalf of the South. Certain other able-bodied men in the Keys felt just as impassioned as Watson and were ready to join the rebellion. Local clerk Alfred B. Lowe and his friends, including Watson, applied for the necessary passes to leave Key West.[80] The Union authorities, aware of pro-Southern sympathies among part of the population, were not about to let them simply quit the island and join the ranks of the enemy. The new commanding officer, Major French, demanded that they swear an oath of allegiance to the Union. This the group of pro-Rebel Key West men would not do, and their applications were therefore denied.

If Major French believed he had outwitted the Key Westers, he was very much mistaken. In the previous month, Confederate hopes had been buoyed by a victory at the Battle of Wilson's Creek in Missouri. Throughout the South, enthusiasm for "the Cause" was running high. Not only did a number of Key West men feel called to serve in the Confederate military, but they also knew the surroundings seas as intimately as any men alive and had connections at the wharves and among sailors and captains. Major French's heavy-handed tactics provoked these Key Westers into setting out on the greatest adventure of their lives.

That September, Robert Watson, fellow Bahamian William Oliver Sawyer, Italian Marcus Oliveri and Peter A. Crusoe, the oldest at forty-one years and previously the clerk of the circuit court at Key West, managed to stow away aboard a British ship. Given Watson's subsequent diary entries, it's clear that the men could only have done this with the collusion of the captain, who may very well have been sympathetic to their cause. (The men went on land without difficulty when the ship anchored in various harbors, something they could hardly have done without both captain and crew becoming aware.) On September 27, Watson recorded that "I left today in the schooner *Lady Bannerman* for the Bahama Islands, in the company with Canfield, Sawyer, Lowe and several others. The schooner has on board 55 passengers in all, the most of which are women and children."[81] We don't know whether the men revealed their plans to their families, who would have pressed on them bundles filled with food and money, or whether they left without saying goodbye. Secreted in the *Lady Bannerman*, they sailed from Key West and in the Middle Keys stopped at the small, mostly Conch-settled[82] Knight's Key, where the numerous family of Temple and Mary Pent made their home. Then the *Lady Bannerman* put in at Indian Key (in present-day Islamorada) where Watson gleefully recorded, "I and Eggleston Curry got a lot of whisky; all hands took a drink and proceeded on our voyage."[83]

The journey wasn't all shore leave and drinking. More than once on the voyage Watson fell ill and felt like he might die. Eventually, he and his band spotted the tiny Bahamian isle of Orange Key, and the following day, on October 3, 1861, they "laid to off Sandy Key [Cay]." Here, Watson's hunger got the better of him: "[I] got a lot of conchs and as my appetite was very keen I ate many conchs, stewed conch, fried conch, and roast conch and tapered off on rum."[84] The Key West runaways eventually landed on Bahamian soil, first at Green Turtle Cay and then northeast of Eleuthera at Harbour Island.

Watson and his Key West companions may have experienced a brief moment of jubilation at being on neutral territory, freed from the dictates of U.S. military commanders. But their next move was not necessarily a simple one: how were they going to make it from this tiny Bahamian isle to a Southern town where they could enlist? Some of the Key Westers, including Robert's brother, George Watson, decided first to rest and recuperate on Harbour Island (famous for its unusual pink sand), while Watson and Cyrus Canfield continued on to Nassau. After eight days of waiting for their compatriots in Nassau and "finding that our pockets were getting low," Robert and his friend Canfield decided not to wait any longer. He'd gotten word that his brother and other friends had returned to Key West. So the two of them, Watson and Canfield, "engaged to work our passage in an old leaky schooner bound for Jacksonville, Fla."[85] The journey on such an unreliable boat proved hair raising: "Every little squall our sails would split and ropes give way and then all hands would be busy for three or four hours."[86] Despite the tumultuous journey, with meager rations to sustain them, the two safely arrived in Jacksonville. There Robert boarded for about a week with a Mrs. Donaldson and then took a train headed for Lake City, looking for opportunities to muster in. When the train stopped at a small station, by chance he ran into two fellow Key Westers: Walter Maloney Jr. and, of all people, Henry Mulrennan, the very man who had been exiled from Key West by Union brass that past June.[87]

Encountering Robert Watson, army veteran and native-born Scot Mulrennan started to formulate a plan to keep the Key West men together. In the meantime, Watson returned to Jacksonville to wait for an opening, possibly on a Confederate steamer. But Mulrennan and Malroney weren't the only coincidental encounters. At Jacksonville, Robert Watson experienced a shock when he spotted three familiar faces in town: Key West compatriots William Sawyer, Peter Crusoe and Marcus Oliveri. He could hardly believe that his friends did "step on shore for we thought they were in Key West for we were told in Nassau that they had gone back to that place. They had been landed at Cape Florida [the present-day Miami region] and walked and boated it from there to Enterprise and there took a steamer for Jacksonville where I met them."[88]

The three adventurers from Key West had made their way through difficult, uncleared terrain, either slogging across sand along the coast or through thickets of saw palmettoes and pines in the dense Florida forests, where they might have caught sight of deer and bears. Fortunately, they had found passage aboard a steamer, mostly likely with sympathetic sailors. Major French's denial of their passes had only hardened these Key Westers' resolve to join the Confederacy. It was one thing to risk one's life when battle started, but Watson, Canfield, Lowe, Oliveri and Sawyer had risked a good deal already.

Reunited with three of his comrades, Robert Watson said goodbye to his other friend, Canfield, who promptly signed up for a Confederate-allied blockade-runner, the ironically named *Olive Branch*. Watson and the others bided their time while Mulrennan, a natural-born ringleader, set things into motion. Within a short while, a Mr. Smith had contacted him and told him that "Mr. Mulrennan had sent him to try and ship me together with Olivevus [*sic*] Marcus, Alfred Lowe and Wm. Sawyer in the Coast Guard," which the resourceful Henry Mulrennan was forming.[89] Soon the Key Westers found themselves traveling to Cedar Keys on the Gulf of Mexico to enlist in the Florida Volunteer Coast Guard Company, reporting to Captain Henry Mulrennan. Fellow Key Wester Walter Maloney Jr., son of Union man Walter Maloney Sr., served as his lieutenant. Then Robert Watson had to walk from Clear Water Harbor to Tampa, about thirty-five miles by his reckoning, but at last the company was taking shape. Soon it became like a regular Key West reunion.

Their company of Key West men, along with others from Florida, found themselves stationed at the backwater Point Pinellas on Tampa Bay, just in time for Christmas. On December 24, the newly enlisted coast guardsmen christened a thirty-foot boat named the *Mollie Post*, as Robert Watson described: "Launched our second boat and had a jolly time of it. Mr. Post requested Mr. Maloney to name her Mollie Post [after his young daughter], which was done. He bought down a lot of whiskey and we launched the boat with Mr. Crusoe and little Mollie Post in her. When the boat was in the water Mr. Crusoe gave us a short but very appropriate speech after which we all took a drink." On Christmas Day, they toasted to the holiday with eggnog. Despite the celebratory atmosphere, there was a more sober reality. If this collection of Key West friends had set sail during the holidays, it might have taken a day and half at sea, more or less, to reach Key West Harbor and be reunited with their wives, mothers, fathers, sisters and bothers. But Key West may as well have been situated on the moon, as Union forces held the island, while they now camped—as enlisted men—in Confederate Florida.

With three ships—the gaff-rigged sailing sloop *Kate Dale*, the largest at approximately eighty feet,[90] and the more modestly sized *Mary Jane* and *Mollie Post*—Mulrennan and the guardsmen patrolled the shore as they scanned the waters for signs of enemy craft.[91] Federal ships might create a blockade of a strategically important harbor; the company's mission was to ensure that Tampa Bay and other surrounding coastal outposts did not suffer a blockade (or capture, as had occurred in Key West). The vessels also assisted in the transport of officers and cannons.[92] For the time being, they were somewhat left to their own devices on the Florida coastal frontier. Robert Watson reported them building their own barracks out of palmettoes and then laboriously digging a well "which caved in as soon as it was dug."[93]

For a short period, Mulrennan and his men enjoyed relative freedom. One evening, the coast guard recruits gathered around the campfire "playing music, singing, dancing, spinning yarns." Washing clothes, target practice, drill practice and gathering oysters to supplement their basic fare filled their days. Occasional treats of beer or wine lightened the men's spirits. At one point, Robert learned that his friend Cyrus Canfield's ship had been captured by Union forces and Cyrus himself taken prisoner. He even received a letter from his brother, George, who had returned to Key West. The young man's attitudes toward the world around him gradually emerge in his diary: one day, Robert and the others seized an older gentleman named Pratt, who "was living with a Negro woman that cooked for the officers." The interracial relationship apparently infuriated the white Key Westers. They threw Pratt bodily off a wharf into the bay and warned that "if he was caught doing the like again that we would give him thirty nine lashes."[94]

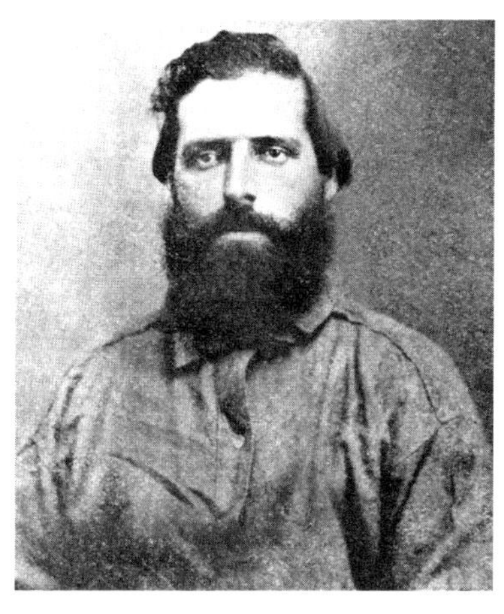

Key Wester John T. Lowe served in Mulrennan's volunteer Florida Coast Guard. *Courtesy of the State Archives of Florida.*

Besides Watson and his friends who had left on the *Lady Brannerman* (Sawyer, Crusoe, Alfred Lowe and Oliveri), there were other Key Westers serving in Mulrennan's volunteer coast guard company: Walter Maloney Jr., Joseph Fagan, Charles H. Berry, John T. Pent, Samuel Morgan, John T. Lowe and the Spaniard Manuel Francisco Diaz. The names of these Key West Confederates all appear in Jefferson Browne's classic chronicle, *Key West: The Old and the New*; additional Key Westers appear to have served with Mulrennan in this early coast guard as well, such as John Russell,[95] Samuel Young Sawyer,[96] Joseph S. Bartlum (son of one of Key West's finest shipbuilders),[97] William D. Curry,[98] Benjamin Albury (or Alberry)[99] and seventeen-year-old Joseph (or Josephus) Moss.[100] A few of the Key Westers had relocated to other Florida settlements before the outbreak of war and joined Mulrennan's company,[101] including the curiously named Augustus Azariah Archer, William Brownell Meares and George Victor Rickards.[102] (Just after Robert Watson joined Mulrennan's coast guard, he wrote wryly in his diary, "Called on Gus Archer, Dicks Mars, John Lowe and some more Key West unfortunates. They were all very glad to see us and treated us like brothers."[103])

In January 1862, on the shore of Point Pinellas, the assembled men adopted a fierce nickname for their company. The new moniker may well have been aimed like a hard slap in the face to Major French, the Union officer who tried to stop them leaving their island home: they were now the "Key West Avengers."[104]

Perhaps the islanders had not been able to defend their home against Union seizure and occupation; perhaps, unlike in Savannah or Charleston, they had not been able to enlist in their hometown, where they might have been sent off to war with parades and music as they waved goodbye in uniforms that their mothers and sisters had sewn by hand. But here, farther north on Florida's coast, they were primed to avenge what these Confederate enlistees saw as a great calamity: Union control of the Florida Keys.

The Confederacy needed men and organization, and the Key West Avengers were not permitted to monitor Florida's central Gulf of Mexico in their three craft, the *Kate Dale*, *Mary Jane* and *Mollie Post*, for long. In late April, "the company known as the Key West Avengers, and commanded by Capt. Henry Mulrenan, at Tampa Bay" was specifically mentioned in a letter to Florida governor John Milton as one of the companies "ordered to be mustered into Confederate service."[105]

Captain Mulrennan and his fellow officer, Second Lieutenant (later Captain) Smith, were charged with leading the men as they were absorbed into Company K in the 7th Florida Infantry. The days of patrolling the Gulf of Mexico ended; the short-lived Key West Avengers would be dispersed, and many of the Key Westers would now see intense action.

Yet the Key Westers' appointment into the 7th Florida Infantry did not sit well with them: they were sailors, wreckers and ship carpenters and felt it would be a waste to have them trudging through the countryside when the Confederate navy faced fierce sea battles, requiring special nautical skills that they possessed in abundance. The men gathered together, and Peter Crusoe composed a petition to the secretary of the Confederate navy that asked they might be mustered into the navy instead. It just so happened that the secretary was a Key West man himself, Stephen Mallory. (As connections went, this was a fine one.) Twenty-five men, referring to themselves as "Citizens of Key West, Fla.," respectfully signed a petition on May 1, 1862:

> *They are sincerely anxious to render good and efficient service to their country and are satisfied that the Army is not the proper place for them, that they have been informed that Seamen in the Army can be transferred to the Navy, and therefore make this their application, and pray to be transferred to a Gun Boat or other vessel of war where they may have a chance to meet the enemy and strike for their Country's cause.*[106]

To a degree, the petition persuaded Mallory. Charles Berry, Samuel Morgan, John Sands and others went into the navy. (Robert Watson, whose skill had helped his leaky transport stay afloat from the Bahamas to Jacksonville, was not transferred to the navy until 1864.) Certain Key West Avengers could remain at sea but now aboard other ships—sometimes with a familiar face, but in other cases mixed in with a crew of strangers far from home.

Captain Smith and Lieutenant Maloney would lead the Key Westers into battle on land; here Henry Mulrennan momentarily disappears from the

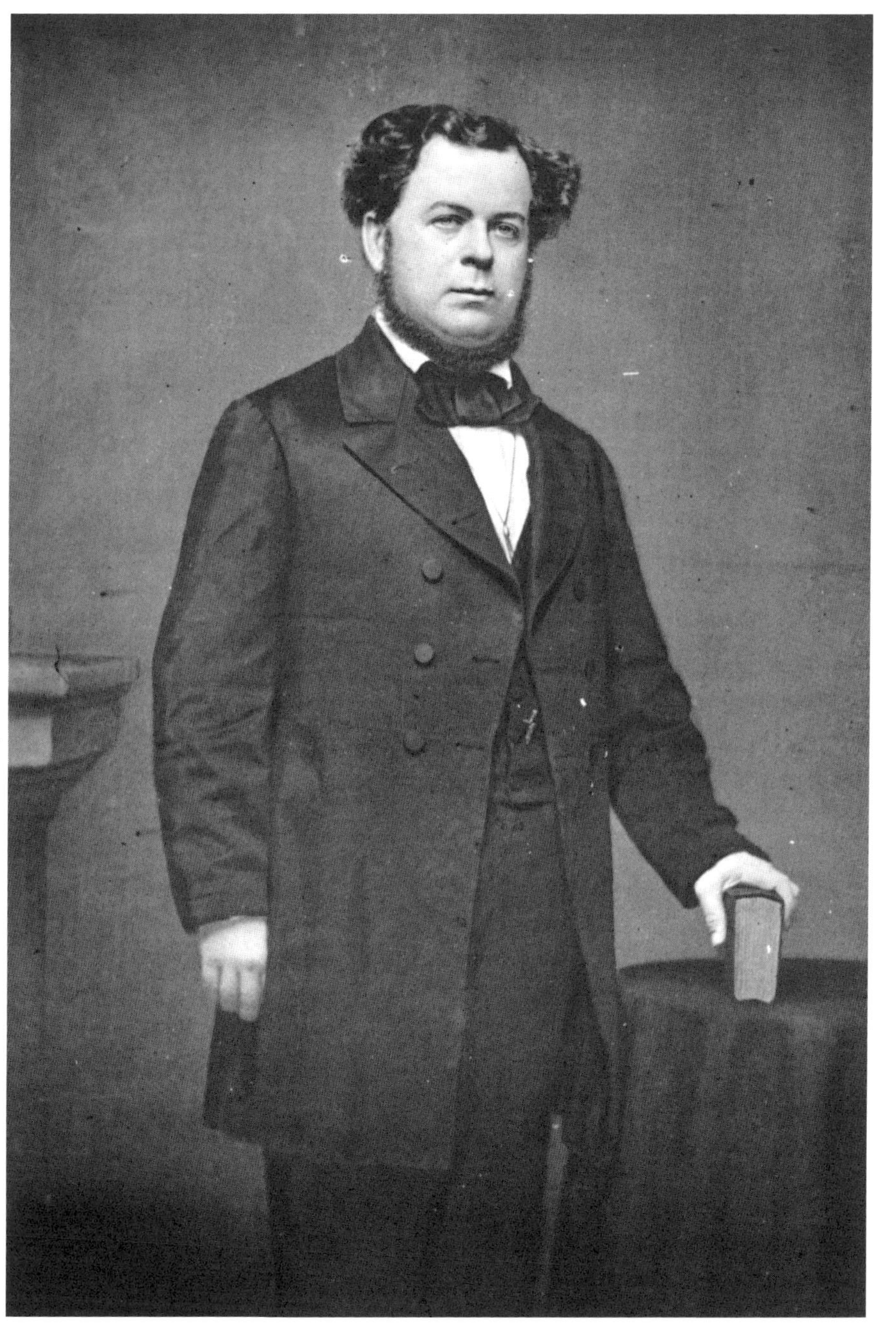

Key Wester Stephen Mallory became secretary of the Confederate navy. *Courtesy of the Monroe County Public Library, Key West.*

record again. After all his efforts to gather his island compadres together on the Gulf Coast of Florida, the Scottish shopkeeper and war veteran did not join Robert Watson and Company K on their long march to Knoxville, Tennessee. Instead, Mulrennan sailed back to waters he knew so well. Robert Watson heard the news that "Mulrennan, Coste, and Marcus have run the blockade to Havana in two smacks [fishing boats]. They left here on the 8th of January and I have heard that they arrived safe in Havana."[107]

Just as quickly as the company formed, the Avengers vanished with nary a trace, swallowed up by the Confederate war machine. For sure, some of the men remained together in the Company K, 7th Florida Infantry, but it would never be the same. What began like a chapter from a boy's adventure story, with stowing away and singing by the campfire, morphed into a difficult war. Watson's diary describes illness, near starvation and scenes of barely contained chaos. For him at least, there was very little glory.

As we look back at those Key West men who went to such great lengths to fight for the Confederacy, one of the most surprising commonalities is how many of them were foreign-born. Mulrennan hailed from chilly Scotland; Crusoe was born in Gibraltar and Marcus Oliveri in Genoa, Italy. Yet a majority of the Key Westers serving in the Key West Avengers hailed from the Bahamas.[108] It initially can strike one as strange that these immigrants from nearby islands risked their lives for the South.

Both white and black Bahamians settled in the Florida Keys from the 1820s onward and helped to mold the population's essential character. After Lincoln was elected in 1860, a number of white Bahamians showed a strong affinity for the South. They may have had varying reasons to pledge their loyalty to the Confederacy, including issues of states' rights and taxation. And then there is the issue of slavery, an institution that had already been abolished in the Bahamas. How did the white Conchs who enlisted with the Confederacy feel about slavery, and did it factor into their decision to enlist?

In 1834, the formal abolition of slavery throughout the British West Indies took place, although an "apprenticeship" system (essentially slavery by another name) lasted until 1838. It would be a mistake, however, to imagine that white Bahamians and black Bahamians responded to this news with similar emotions. For enslaved people, this turn of events meant freedom and was a cause for great celebration. For most West Indian whites—including those in the Bahamas—abolition meant a sometimes drastic change to their economies and, perhaps more compellingly, a fundamental upheaval in the social order. Decades after abolition, even poor whites in the Bahamas "despite their poverty, despised nonwhites."[109] In fact, "well into the twentieth century the white [Bahamian] elite controlled the political, social, and economic life of the colony,"[110] and "the system of racial discrimination inherited from the institution of enslavement persisted into the 1960s."[111] As Bahamian scholar Gail Saunders has documented, for well over a century after abolition, racial tensions in the Bahamas mirrored "the inflexible color line of the United States."[112]

Emancipation in the Bahamas had not resulted in whites learning to accept blacks as fellow citizens or equals; on the contrary, whites' contempt for blacks remained and, in some cases, perhaps intensified, as their resentment of these now-emancipated people of color grew. (This development would be echoed in the post–Civil War South, when white Southern antipathy toward blacks increased.) White Bahamians who immigrated to the Florida Keys in the antebellum period would not have harbored any special sympathy toward blacks or necessarily supported black emancipation; some may have found comfort in living in a new land where the old social order of a slave society was still entrenched. Even in the Bahamas' colonial motherland, Great Britain, there was plenty of support for the Confederacy. In reality, "substantial sections of Britain's business elite were working with impunity to help the slave-owning southern states win the Civil War—despite the fact that Britain was officially neutral and had outlawed slavery almost 30 years earlier."[113]

As incredible as it may seem to us today, in the English-speaking world outside the South, there were many who either tolerated or supported the old order and loathed the idea of social change. Robert Watson, born on Ragged Island in the Bahamas, had arrived in Key West with his parents in 1847 to find a place where certain leading citizens owned slaves as a matter of course. Up until 1838, black enslavement had been the way of things in his homeland as well. On Ragged Island, slaves had tended to the profitable salt ponds.[114] Meanwhile, at least 4 of Watson's Key West Avenger comrades had been born on tiny Green Turtle Cay, where, as of 1834, white Bahamians—including those with last names Russell, Curry, Sawyer and Lowe—owned 241 black men, women and children.[115] Having witnessed relatives and neighbors lose valuable "property" due to emancipation in the Bahamas, white Conchs may have felt determined not to allow the same thing happen in Florida.

In the published version of his diary, however, Watson does not comment on slavery, although his hatred of Yankees and "Lincolnites" is clear, and he particularly objected to being housed with "Negro soldiers" when the war was over. (Most white Union troops would have felt the same.) Did Watson,

Alfred Lowe and the other Conchs who mustered into the CSA and the CSN support slavery, or were there other motivating factors? That history still waits to be uncovered. One fact is certain: Although there may have been white Bahamians in the Florida Keys who felt pro-Union, at the outbreak of the Civil War it appears that a number of them allied themselves politically, culturally and emotionally with the Confederate States of America.

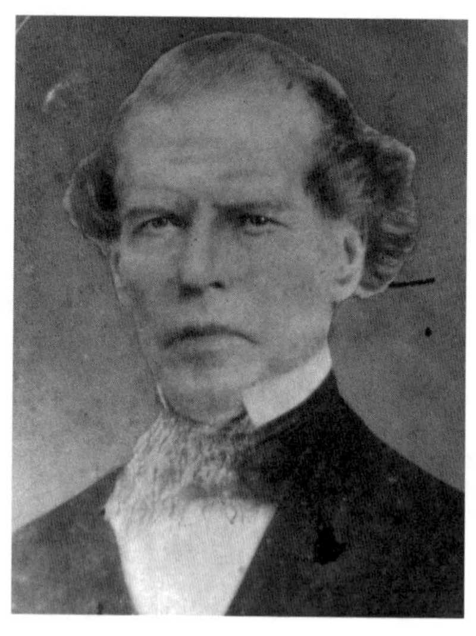

Walter Maloney Sr. was a staunch pro-Union man; his son fought on behalf of the Confederacy. *Courtesy of the Monroe County Public Library, Key West.*

Of course, the short-lived Key West Avengers were not the only Confederates to emerge from the Florida Keys. Some of these other stories, such as that of merchant Asa Tift, are better known; one also cannot overlook the pro-Union citizens who found the idea of secession illegal and traitorous. Their stories are hardly hidden history either: Walter Maloney Sr., who supported the Union from the beginning, and Judge William Marvin, who punished blockade-runners in court, are just two examples. Many Key Westers eventually signed an oath of allegiance to the United States, some because they had always thought secession wrong and others because they realized which way the winds of war were blowing. Even those with pro-Union leanings often had a deep prejudice about their black neighbors, however. A Northern colored regiment eventually served in Key West and found its welcome less than warm. The complex Civil War history of the Florida Keys could fill a long volume.[116]

In the end, what exactly happened to those tenacious Keys men who risked their lives for a Lost Cause? Charles Berry died in 1863 in the explosion of the CSS *Chattahochee*. William Sawyer died early in his service, in 1863, and was buried in Tennessee. William D. Curry contracted malaria during his service and stated on his Confederate pension application in 1886 that he had never recovered from the disease. Peter Crusoe's career as a Confederate did not impede his standing in Key West: after the war, he resumed his position as clerk of the circuit court. Walter Maloney Jr. returned to his island city, reconciled with his pro-Union father and served a term as mayor. Manuel Diaz returned to Key West, married a woman named Ascunsion and lived until 1910. Despite being shot in the hand, John Pent also survived the war and settled back in Key West, where he wed Elizabeth Bowe; they would die in 1919 within a month of each other. Another man who returned to Key West safely was Joseph Bartlum, who eventually passed away in his sixties. Key Westers Alfred Lowe and John Thomas Lowe participated in the dramatic scuttling of the CSS *Savannah*, before General Sherman seized that eponymous Southern city; Alfred lived in Key West until his death in 1921, while John settled on the Florida Gulf Coast and died not far from where the Avengers first camped. Henry Mulrennan, Rebel firebrand and later Confederate blockade-runner, lived through the Civil War and went on to serve as Key West mayor for two years. Today, visitors to the Key West cemetery will find a Confederate marker atop his grave.

Diarist and onetime stowaway Robert Watson was captured by Union troops in Virginia, one day before Lee's surrender at Appomattox. As a prisoner in Washington, D.C., he recorded, "I don't want to take the Oath [of Allegiance to the United States] but if they send me to prison I will take it for I am satisfied that the South has gone up the spout and it is of no use

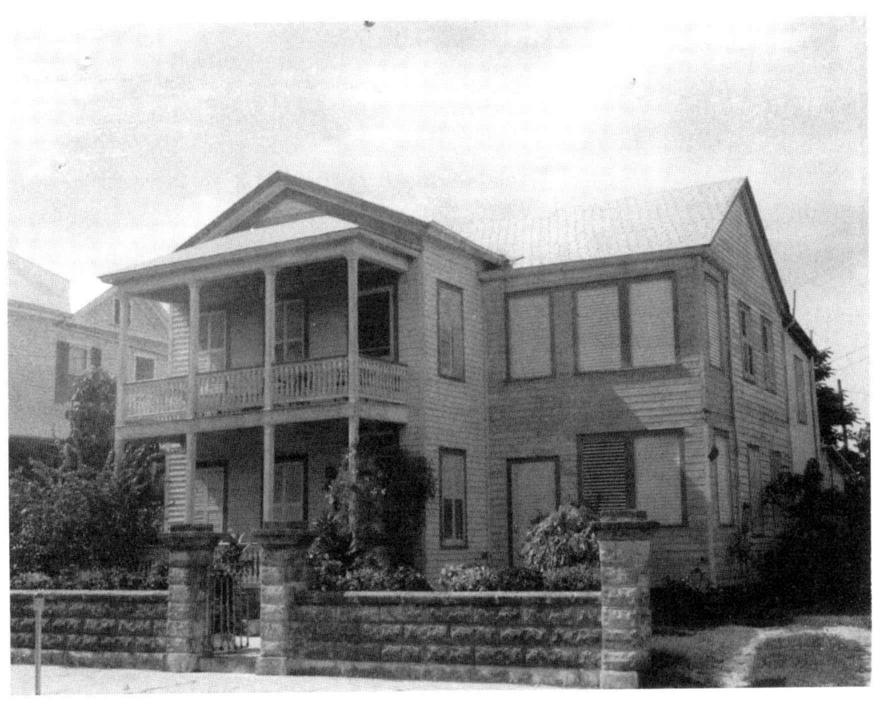

Confederate veteran Robert Watson built this house at 522 Simonton Street in about 1869. *Courtesy of the Monroe County Public Library, Key West.*

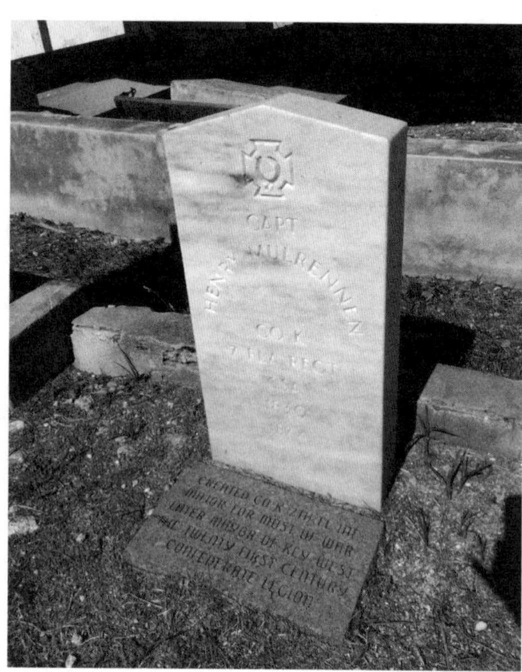

Henry Mulrennan's grave site in the Key West Cemetery. *Photograph by Laura Albritton.*

for me to linger for a long time in prison for no purpose."[117] Having written that, Watson nonetheless refused to sign the oath yet still managed to get paroled and returned to Key West. His diary, published in the twenty-first century, attests to the mundane horrors of war, including near starvation and disease. In one typical passage, he wrote, "Nothing to eat but we are all well supplied with lice." Another evening, he recorded, "Mud ankle deep and not a wink of sleep. Stopped raining at midnight when we stripped off and dried our clothes by the fire. All hands as hungry as wolves and nothing to eat." The Key West Avengers' grand adventure, which had begun in high spirits, turned into a grim, relentless slog.

As Watson, Lowe and others trickled back to their homes within a once again united United States, more than 600,000 men lay dead. Almost 4 million men, women and children of color were now freed of their shackles, and an assassin had murdered one of the greatest American presidents to ever live. The world that some had hoped to preserve in amber had changed. After all the tragedy, the deaths, the strange adventures and sleeping out under unfamiliar skies far from home, there was nothing left to avenge. Those who survived returned to their lives and carried on.

Chapter 4

A Town of Their Own

In 1890, a tall, young black man named George Adderley surveyed his island home of New Providence in the Bahamas and knew that it was time to leave. Nassau, with its crush of people, was too crowded, and the beautiful bays, inlets and beaches of the twenty-one-square-mile isle were not enough to keep him in the Bahamas. Few opportunities existed on New Providence for the twenty-year-old, especially if he wanted to own his own land. Instead, George would seek his fortune in South Florida. Like many immigrants to America, he took little with him save for the skills he had honed and a sense of ambition. In a small boat, he and his young wife, Olivia, sailed across the Gulf Stream and headed for a sparsely inhabited group of islands: the Upper Florida Keys.

What George and Olivia discovered on the Matecumbes resembled much of the Bahamas: islands that poked a bit above sea level, surrounded by clear, turquoise ocean with plentiful conch and fish. Palm trees added color to the landscape, while egrets perched on the mangroves like so many tufts of white cotton. Very few people dared to settle on islands so remote, with limited or no fresh water. Miami, still just a backwater in 1890, lay about ninety miles away, while Key West was more than seventy miles. Yet Conchs from the Bahamas already knew how to survive in these trying conditions; they knew which fruit trees and vegetables to plant in the meager soil and how to wrest dinner from the sea. They understood how to use what they found: palm fronds for roof thatch and driftwood that the tide brought in.

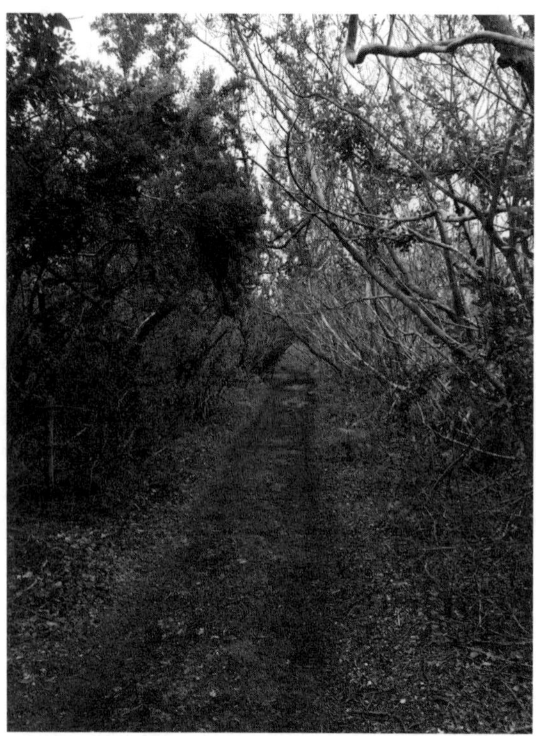

The tropical hammock at Crane Point, where George and Olivia Adderley settled. *Photograph by Laura Albritton.*

Like his mainly white neighbors in the Upper Keys, George Adderley also brought with him a streak of resolute independence. Key West—with its busy shops, wharves and streets—held no attraction for him. The 1900 U.S. census reported that George and Olivia made their home on lonely Upper or Lower Matecumbe with a cousin, Virginia Rand.[118] For more than ten years, George worked the sea and also found employment as a farm laborer in a region that could aptly be described as "the middle of nowhere." Most importantly, he managed to save part of his earnings.

Boats were the only mode of transportation along the Keys, and by sailing up and down the island chain, George grew to know Key Vaca, to the south in the Middle Keys. A white woman, Annie Crain, had inherited the island from a relative, Horatio Crain, and began to sell off parcels of land in the early twentieth century. This is when George and Olivia's frugality paid off: in 1903, George bought thirty-two acres from Annie Crain for $100, payable over three years.[119]

Located on the north side of Key Vaca, these acres had attracted a small group of black Bahamian settlers. Whites lived on Key Vaca as well, but at a distance. From the beginning, as George and Olivia set about building a new life for themselves, they made a choice to keep among their own race. This strategy was understandable, given the harsh social and political realities of the Jim Crow era. The Adderleys' acreage was set in dense tropical hammock, within a section of land called Crane Point, and looked out over Florida Bay—porpoises flashed by some mornings, while in wintertime, gentle, bulbous manatees appeared frequently. Barely separated from Crane Point by a tiny inlet lay Rachel Key,[120] where black settlers established themselves as well. Only George Adderley owned his own land, however, and only George among them could read; as a result, he emerged as the community's natural leader.

George and Olivia had apparently had sons, but tragically, they died young. The couple then adopted a girl, Louisa Smith, and started to put down roots on the new property.[121] In addition to caring for Louisa, Olivia would have spent her days gathering and chopping firewood for cooking; picking cantaloupes and sapodillas; harvesting sweet potatoes from their kitchen garden; tending to livestock such as pigs, chickens and goats; making lye soap; cleaning house; cooking meals in the outdoor kitchen; and washing laundry by hand. The other settler women, such as Margaret Curry, wife of Joseph, spent their days doing similar tasks. To ward off the mosquitoes and no-see-ums that swarmed in the Middle Keys, they burned smudge fires, which felt oppressively hot in summertime.

Meanwhile, George Adderley and other male members of the black community went sponging. To harvest sponges, they would stand up in their small boats to spot the sponges on the seafloor or crouch down and use a glass-bottomed bucket to peer into the water. They ensnared the sponges with long poles affixed with three metal hooks. Sponges were living things and had to be dried out thoroughly. (During the drying process, they smelled horrible.) Once George and the others accumulated enough dried sponges, they sailed for Key West to sell them at market. These trips brought them income, which they could use to purchase necessities such as flour and fabric.

Five families of black settlers (about eighteen people in total) lived on Rachel Key, including a man named Joseph Rigby. At some point, people began calling the settlement of Crane Point and Rachel Key "Adderley Town." All the Adderley Town residents hailed from the Bahamas except for one couple, David and Janet Freeman, who had migrated from South Carolina.[122] Three black men from the community didn't make their home on land at all but rather lived aboard a schooner. All told, the total numbered just under thirty souls.

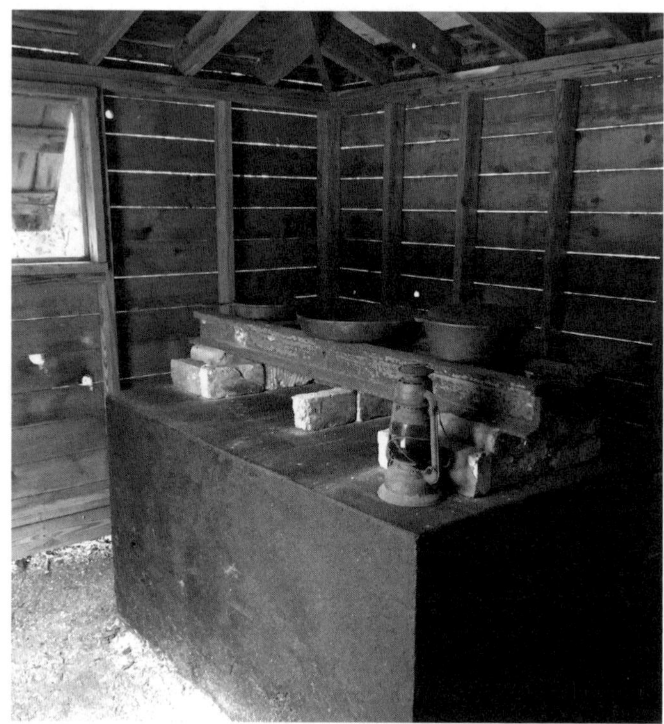

The kitchen, which stands at a distance from the Adderley House. *Photograph by Laura Albritton.*

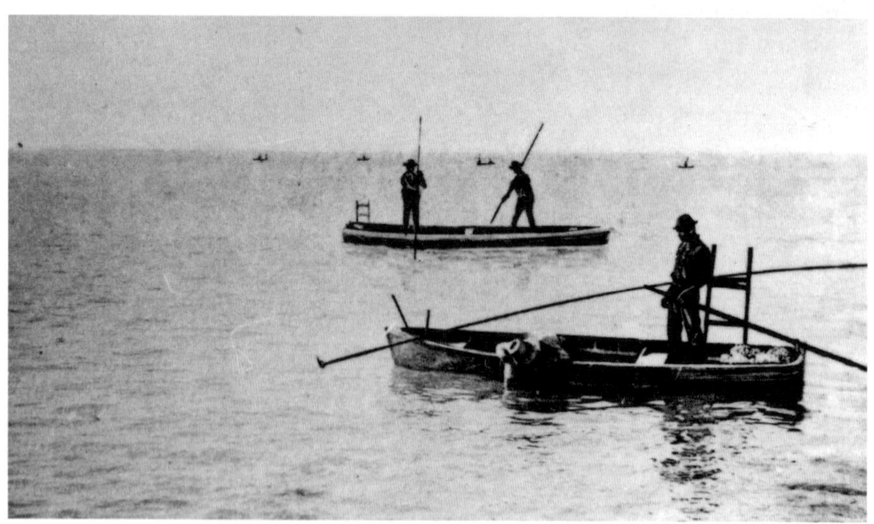

Spongers searching the ocean floor in the Keys. *Courtesy of the Monroe County Public Library, Key West.*

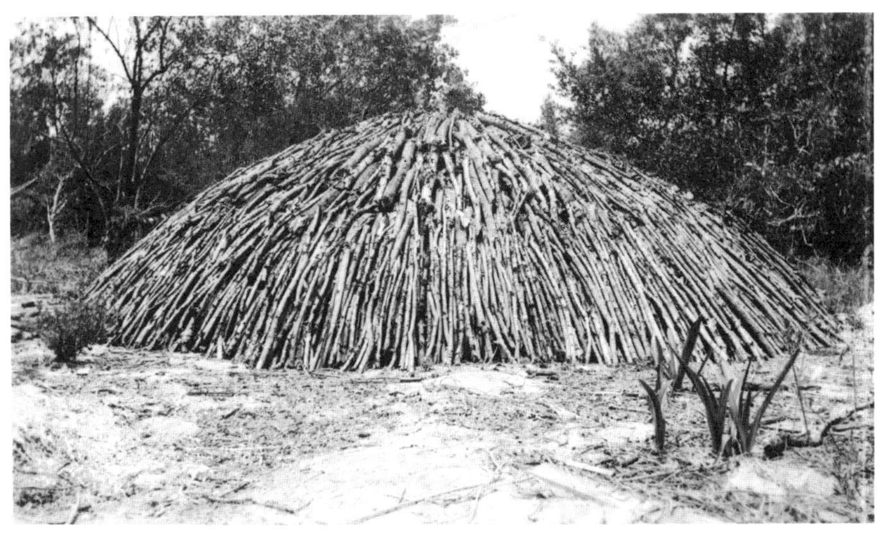

A charcoal kiln in the Florida Keys. Adderley Town residents constructed kilns like this one to produce charcoal. *Courtesy of the Monroe County Public Library, Key West.*

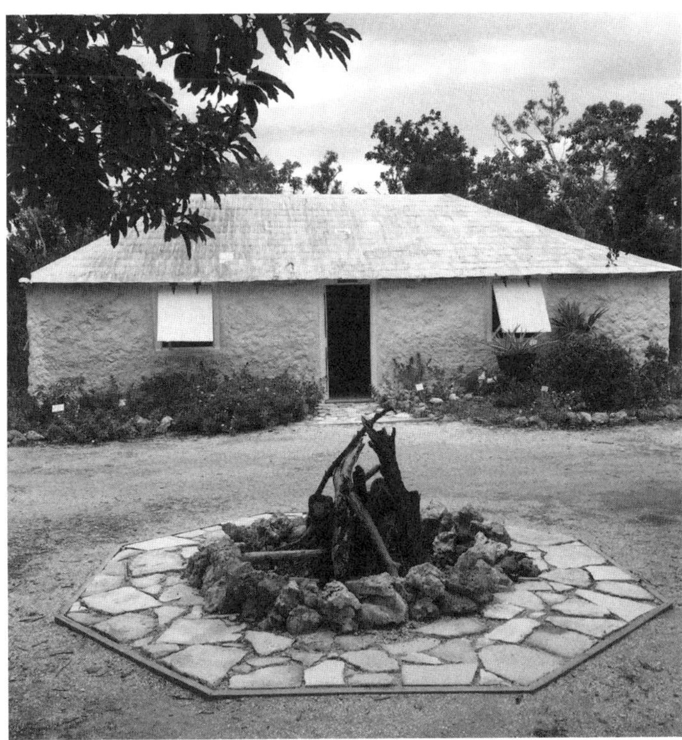

The house that George and Olivia Adderley built of tabby still stands. *Photograph by Laura Albritton.*

In addition to sponging and fishing, the men of Adderley Town made charcoal. At the time, charcoal was a much-desired commodity, and in Key West, it could bring a handsome profit. The process required stamina and physical strength. First, the men had to cut down a quantity of buttonwood trees and prepare the wood for a fire. Then they stacked wood in a giant cone and put sand and grass over it to "to make it airtight," as historian Charleton Tebeau chronicled, with a vent at the very top. Working with fire could be dangerous, and along with mosquitoes, tropical heat guaranteed that charcoal-making was hot, hard toil.

When it came time for George and Olivia to build a house, they thought back to the Bahamas and to structures that had withstood hurricanes. The couple decided to build their house of tabby. This strong building material is similar to concrete and is made by burning shells.[123] Tabby was used throughout the West Indies[124] and also in coastal Georgia and South Carolina. Sometime between 1904 and 1906, the Adderleys constructed their twenty-one- by thirty-foot home, crushing local shells and burning them at high temperatures to extract the lime; they also implanted whole conch shells in the walls. Standing one story high, the rectangular structure originally had a palm thatch roof. Windows provided ventilation, while simple shutters could be closed to repel rain, wind and, to some extent, the dreaded mosquitoes.

The tabby Adderley house differed from other residents' wooden homes and indeed was unlike anything else in the entire Florida Keys. It was a proud, sturdy structure destined to survive. Their house would come to serve as the center of this isolated black community. George and Olivia had created, if not a paradise, then a true town of their own—a remarkable accomplishment for two black Bahamian immigrants in the early 1900s.

But their peace and tranquility could not last forever. Standard Oil millionaire Henry Flagler had ambitions to fashion an Overseas Railroad that would connect the Florida mainland with Key West. For the project's headquarters, Flagler and his railway staff chose the Middle Keys. Soon engineers, laborers, accountants and cooks descended on the islands. The sounds of dredging, hammering and soldering overtook the quiet. Engineers even built a tennis court and an athletic club to keep themselves entertained. The Florida East Coast Railway began to construct a temporary trestle to Knight's Key Dock that would allow the train to meet ships, which then whisked passengers away to the delights of Cuba. There was only one problem: the railroad needed right-of-way across George Adderley's land.

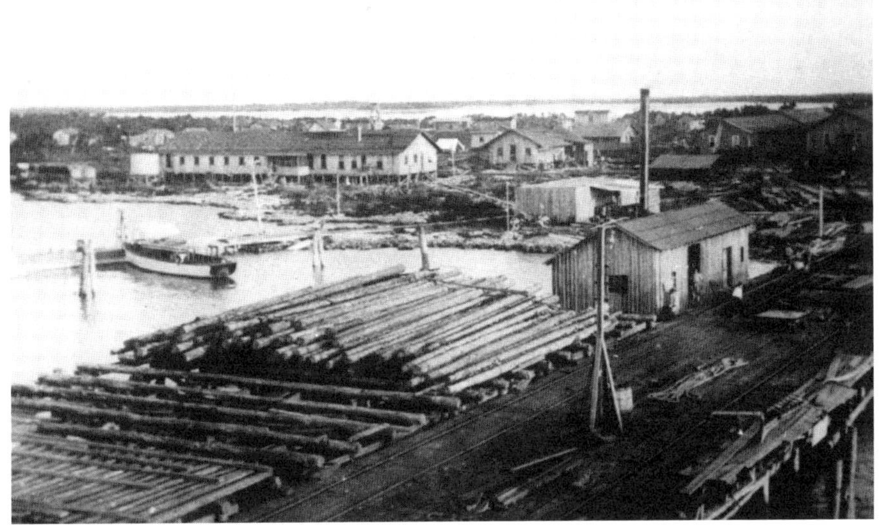

The FEC Railway constructed Work Camp No. 10, which later became known as Marathon. *Courtesy of the Monroe County Public Library, Key West.*

A black immigrant of modest means might have been no match for the all-powerful Henry Flagler, and certainly he would not have been if, like his fellow townspeople, George Adderley had not held a deed to the land. But he did, and that provided leverage. In exchange for giving the FEC right-of-way, Adderley Town got its own stop on the Overseas Railroad.

"Vaca" did not have an elaborate depot but rather a simple platform with a flag that could be lowered when passengers wanted a ride. While Vaca Station did not appear on the official FEC timetables, about once per week this flag appeared, and the train stopped to take on Adderley Town passengers headed to Homestead or Miami.[125] Their obscure town now had a rail connection with the rest of the world.

"Marathon" became the new name of the FEC headquarters on Key Vaca, and for a time, it was a busy town with wood-frame homes, docks, warehouses, a little school, a clinic, a hotel and other amenities. But once work finally wrapped up in 1916, most of the FEC workers and their families moved on. The few railroad employees who remained lived, for the most part, on Pigeon Key. Once again, Key Vaca shrank to an isolated outpost, but at least one that had a rail connection with Miami and Key West. In 1917, certain black Bahamians named Adderley who lived in Monroe County enlisted in the civilian draft for World War I; they may have been

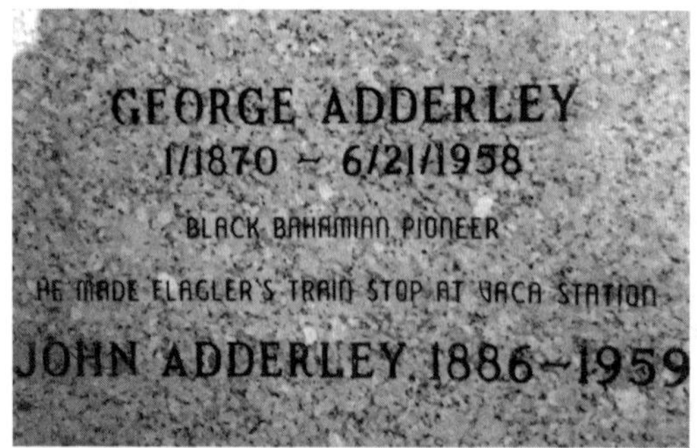

George Adderley's gravestone at the Key West Cemetery. *Photograph by Laura Albritton.*

nephews of George and Olivia's. But otherwise, Adderley Town residents continued with their lives much as before. For the next decades, they fished, worked their land and kept mainly to themselves.

Finally, time caught up with the little town. In July 1950, Olivia Adderley passed away. It must have been a terrible blow to lose his life's companion, because after that, George Adderley made drastic changes. He sold the acreage, which had belonged to him for almost fifty years, to a wealthy white couple, Francis and Mary Crane. The Cranes built an impressive house on the property, but to their credit, they did not tear down the tabby home that George and Olivia constructed decades before. Adderley Town itself disappeared. George Adderley moved to Key West, which might seem out of character, until one considers where he spent the last years of his life—at a home for the blind.[126] At some point in his seventies, he had begun to lose his sight. Olivia was buried (or possibly reburied) at the Key West Cemetery, and when George died in 1958, he was buried there alongside her. No stone or plaque marked their graves for many years. Two early pioneers of the Florida Keys might have been forgotten, their accomplishments lost.

But historians knew that the oldest surviving house in the Florida Keys—outside of Key West—was the one these two black Bahamians had constructed on Key Vaca. Historians also realized that to found a town and establish an independent black community was something that should be commemorated. The Crane Point Museum and Nature Center in Marathon preserved the site and, more recently, oversaw an extensive restoration of the Adderley House. Visitors can walk inside the dwelling, stroll by the outdoor kitchen and medicinal garden and learn about George, Olivia and the town that grew up around them.[127] To ensure that they are further remembered, the Historic Florida Keys Foundation commissioned stone plaques for the couple in the Key West Cemetery. George's grave now reads, "Black Bahamian Pioneer. He made Flagler's train stop at Vaca Station."

Chapter 5

The Great Key West Extension Scare

It sounds like the premise for a fantastical novel: A millionaire dreams up the scheme for a train that travels clear across far-flung islands, chugging away on tracks laid over man-made fill and soaring high above the aqua-blue ocean on bridges that span miles. The millionaire was, of course, Standard Oil co-founder Henry Morrison Flagler, and the islands in question were the stunningly tropical yet mostly undeveloped Florida Keys, at the very southernmost latitudes of the United States. For hundreds of years, these "keys"—rocky outposts dotted with palms and red-barked gumbo limbo trees—had largely been the dominion of wild seabirds; later, Indian tribal peoples lived here off the abundance of the sea. Then, in the nineteenth century, Key West blossomed into a wealthy frontier town, while small settlements in the Middle Keys and on Indian Key sprang up for a time before fading away.

All that would change with the coming of Henry Flagler's trains—that is, if his people could bring this "Eighth Wonder of the World" to actualization. It was the early twentieth century, an era of grand ambition and breakneck technological innovation. Although some expressed doubt that a railroad running from the southern Florida mainland clear across the islands to Key West could be built, Flagler had confidence that it would.

To accomplish such a seemingly impossible feat, he would need equipment, steel, concrete, fill, workers and brilliant engineers. In the process of building the railroad, Flagler's chief engineer, Joseph Meredith, would literally work himself to death, leaving his principal assistant engineer, William Krome, to

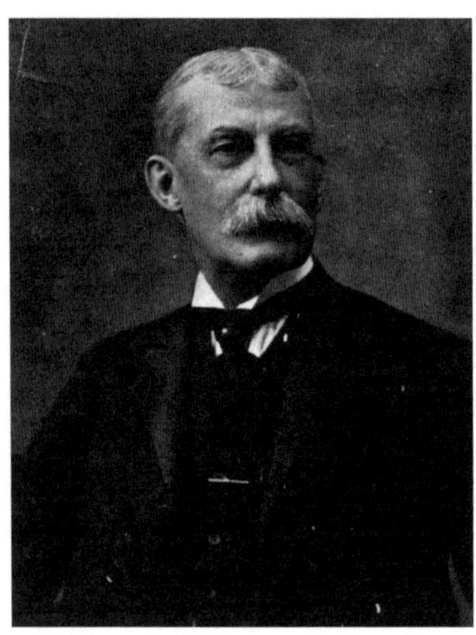

Standard Oil millionaire Henry Flagler believed that the Overseas Railroad would become a reality. *Courtesy of the Monroe County Public Library, Key West.*

see the project through to its completion. But at one point during the long saga of the Overseas Railroad, the scheme would falter. In fact, for two precarious years during its construction, the future of Key West's railroad connection fell into doubt. It was a battle largely hidden from public view, pitting two indomitable forces against each other. Had one side not prevailed, the railroad might have terminated in the Middle Keys, with Key West as isolated as ever.

The technically demanding task of connecting the southeastern Florida mainland with the Florida Keys, carried out under intense sun amid swarms of mosquitoes, started in 1905, with the first stretch running from Florida City to Jewfish Creek. People came to call the project the "Overseas Railroad," but its official title was more of a mouthful: the Florida East Coast Railway's Key West Extension. Industrialist Henry Flagler had already run the Florida East Coast Railway all the way down the state to Miami. He did not intend on furthering the railroad with a link to the Florida Keys out of the goodness of his heart: his goal centered on using his Pacific & Occidental steamers, along with railroad ferries, to run between Havana and Key West; tropical produce from Cuba could be whisked all the way up America's East Coast by rail, while tourists in search of warm weather could ride the rails south to Flagler's hotels along the coast of Florida (and, ultimately, in Key West). As historian Tom Hambright noted, "Miami wasn't a shipping port at the time. The only real natural port in those days was Key West. In 1900, it was Florida's largest city, a bustling port alive with the cigar industry, fishing and sponging. So the impetus for building an overseas railroad was that Henry Flagler needed a port."[128] Yet the implications of a Key West terminal and rail link went well beyond Flagler's own company interests and might have extended to American trade more generally. In early 1907, the *Morning News* predicted that "with these harbor facilities, Key West will almost immediately rank with New Orleans, Mobile, and Galveston as a commercial port."

Two years into construction, in 1907, publicity surrounding the FEC's Key West Extension had ballooned until it was one of the most famous construction endeavors in the United States. The sheer audaciousness of the undertaking fascinated the public. But not everyone admired it—William Randolph Hearst's newspapers attacked "Flagler's Folly." Yet despite its detractors, the work moved ahead steadily. Obstacles that surfaced were overcome with money, skill, cunning or some combination of the three. When a new challenge arose over land usage in Key West, the solution at first seemed straightforward.

Today, Key West has a land area of only 5.27 square miles, but in 1907, the island was even smaller. Obtaining adequate land for the sizeable Key West terminus (final station) and docks remained a major headache for Flagler and his senior staff. And so, Flagler decided with a typically American "can do" attitude to solve the land problem simply: they would create more land. In April, the *St. Louis Globe Democrat* reported on "the vast expense of the improvements at Key West, where it is proposed to fill in 174 acres of land now under water" in order to "build extensive docks and terminals, as well as dry docks and wharves, each 800 feet long and 100 feet wide."[129]

While the railroad construction continued farther north in the Middle Keys, particularly with the Knight's Key Dock (an offshore railroad "terminus" or station out one and a quarter miles into the ocean), the

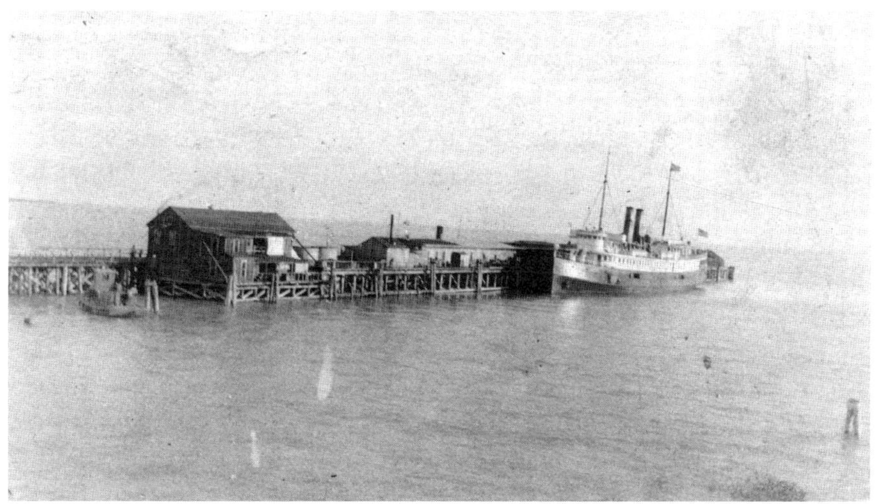

Knight's Key Dock extended to a location with water deep enough for steamships. *Courtesy of the Monroe County Public Library, Key West.*

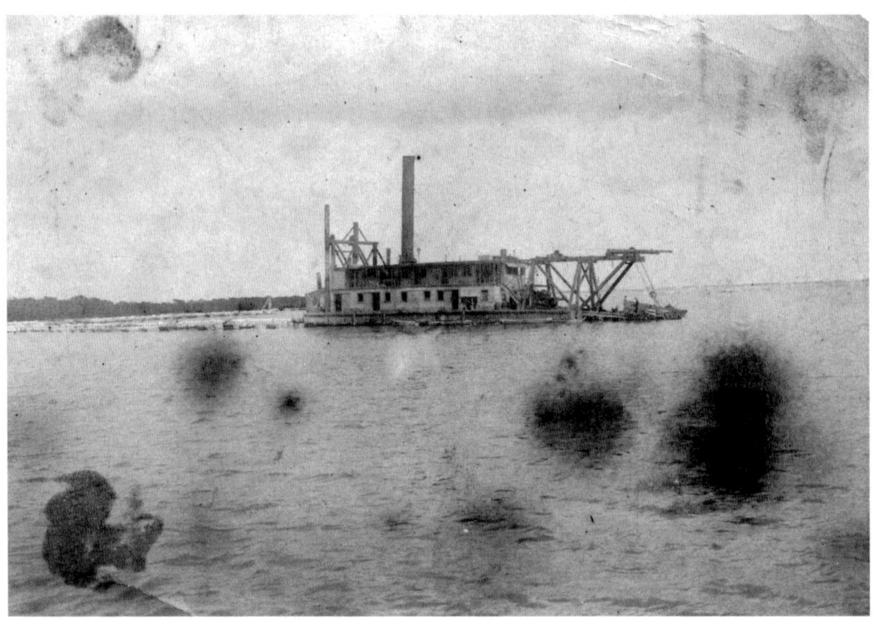

This photograph shows the *George Allen*, one of the dredges Howard Trumbo directed off Key West. *Courtesy of the Monroe County Public Library, Key West.*

project at Key West got underway. The FEC opened up a Key West office, and Howard Trumbo of the Trumbo American Dredging Company directed the huge dredging operation. On October 23, 1906, a dredge called the *George Allen* set to work, bringing forth matter from the ocean floor to create the property that Henry Flagler needed to complete his vision. On November 10, another dredge named the *Grampus* joined it.[130] Things were looking up in Key West. The only serious trouble bedeviling the FEC at that moment was a shortage of workers.

The FEC's construction evaluation reports from 1907 tell the story in numbers: in June of that same year, 2,940 men labored on the project. In the Upper and Middle Florida Keys, they built bridges, laid track and dredged for marine marl.[131] Engineering and accounting staff worked in the FEC offices at Marathon, while a much smaller staff manned the FEC office on Front Street in Key West. Assistant Principal Engineer William Krome kept scrapbooks in which he pasted newspaper articles recording the railway's progress. Krome—a slight, serious-looking man whose staid, buttoned-up appearance belied his tenacity and engineering brilliance—kept one short notice from July 10, 1907: "Mr. H.M. Flagler is expected the latter part of the week to view extension work." The millionaire with the bristly white mustache planned to travel down the east coast of Florida to make a decision about the bridge at Bahia Honda. It seemed that nothing could interfere with the progress of the Overseas Railroad.

Meanwhile, in Key West, the *George Allen* dug up 55,000 cubic yards of fill from July 1 to July 13, while the *Grampus* dredged 1,500 cubic yards of rock in that same period.[132] The first indication that something with the FEC Railway's extension had gone amiss appears in Krome's scrapbook in a small, innocent-looking article from the *Key West Citizen* dated July 15: "Only an Incident: Stoppage of Railroad Work Only Affects Dredges." The newspaper account turned out to be overly optimistic.

Two days later, another report emerged that the U.S. War Department itself had caused the stoppage of the railroad's work. The cause? Allegedly, the War Department and naval authorities halted work "because various channels have been blocked by trestles and viaducts." This explanation may well have struck readers as vague and not terribly convincing. Then, news for Key West's terminal grew worse: a telegram arrived from Howard Trumbo, announcing that both dredges would be "out of commission for several months." The *Key West Citizen*, in a nervous-sounding piece from July 17, related that "[n]o confirmation or denial of the report would be made by Mr. Wilson, in charge of the company's office here today, but it is safe to assume that there is something to the rumor." One day later, the rumor became a concrete reality with an article titled "A Serious Situation: All Work This Side of Knight's Key Suspended."[133]

To say that this news threw many Key Westers into a state of worry would be an understatement. The railroad had become the object of many hopes and dreams, not simply Flagler's. Merchants, housewives, laborers and manufacturers all could benefit in different ways, both large and small, from a rail link with the mainland. Living on a small island located about 150 miles from the American mainland and 90 miles from Havana, many Key Westers perceived their economic progress in the early twentieth century as hampered by its isolation. Henry Flagler's train was destined to be the single most transformative event in the Keys, particularly in Key West, since Spain ceded Florida to the United States—if only the second half of the railroad could be built.

The public did not have to wait long for the U.S. Navy's official reply. In a July 19 *Citizen* article headlined "The Navy's Side," Commodore Beehler, commandant of the naval station at Key West, strongly argued their points. He claimed that Flagler and the FEC had first agreed to sign a contract stating they would eventually replace any fill they dredged at Fleming Key and then reneged. With no contract, the FEC had no right to proceed. Among the most damning was this assertion:

> *Last May, the railroad company, without authority, deliberately began to take material from the U.S. Reservation at Fleming Key. This is Government property and could not be given away by anyone, except by an Act of Congress. No person, not even the Secretary of the Navy, could give Government property to the railroad or anyone without the authority of the people thru Congress.*

The case laid out by the commodore hinged on the notion that the even the sea bottom adjacent to Fleming Key (just north of what is today Trumbo Point) belonged to the United States government. On one hand, one can understand why Flagler and his FEC engineers had not come to the same conclusion: perhaps as far as they were concerned, this material was simply muck, sitting there without purpose in the open ocean. On the other hand, Flagler may very well have believed that the dredging project trespassed onto the navy's territory and blithely ignored this inconvenient truth. He must have imagined, after all, that the Overseas Railroad would benefit everyone in Key West, particularly the military. Perhaps the thought that the navy might object seemed inconceivable.

We can judge Flagler's response to this broadside by what happened next. On July 22, 1907, the company posted a notice that "No More Workers Are Needed."[134] Reports declared that all work camps south of the Middle Keys would be relocated to Knight's Key or farther north. A week later, on July 31, top FEC brass—including Joseph R. Parrott, R.T. Goff and a Mr. Beamis—traveled from St. Augustine and Palm Beach to "assist in reduction of the force," a newspaper reported. As far as Key West was concerned, the news grew even more serious. On August 11, John E. Lummus, who handled the supply system for the railway company, removed $10,000 worth of commissary supplies from Key West and transported them to the terminal dock at Miami.[135] The company also relocated steamers to Miami as work south of Knight's Key wrapped up.

One newspaper reported that Chief Engineer Meredith had sent a telegram calling a halt to all work on the Key West end of the line. The writer pulled no punches in laying blame: "The reason assigned for this action…is that Mr. Flagler has been greatly annoyed and hampered in his great work by obstructions placed in his way by the government, especially the Navy Department."[136] The same article ended on a note of anxiety: "It is sincerely hoped that the trouble may be speedily adjusted, as Key West's future is at stake."

Florida East Coast Railway company officials remained quiet. One rumor emerged that the railroad might stop midway along the island chain, with service onward to Key West only by ship. As far as we know, Flagler and his representatives neither denied nor confirmed the stories, which only fueled speculation and, in some cases, wild rumor. In fact, one paper reported that Flagler was dying of the "grippe" (influenza). Another newspaper, with the dramatic headline "The Coils that Are Crushing H.M. Flagler," asserted that the great man's health was "shattered by the collapse of his costly Key West railroad enterprise." (An illustration of a giant cobra poised to strike a cartoon Flagler added to the sense of impending doom.) "Friendly," pro-Flagler newspapers countered these stories as hearsay, with one paper retorting that the millionaire remained in the "best of health."[137] Meanwhile, news from the southernmost key did not improve. By November, a South Florida paper reported that "the fixtures and supplies of the extension office at Key West have been ordered packed and shipped to this city [Miami] and the office there closed for the present."

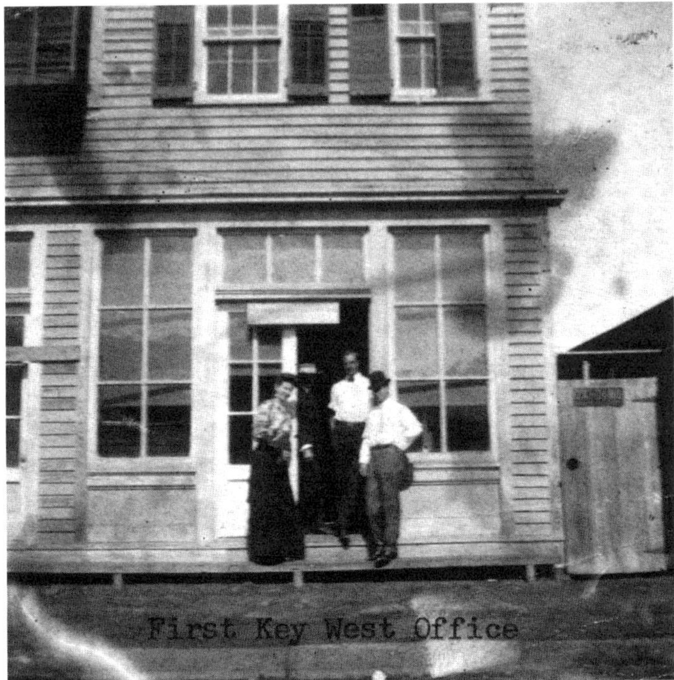

The Florida East Coast Railway's first office in Key West was on Front Street. *Courtesy of the Monroe County Public Library, Key West.*

From Key West's earliest days as an American outpost, the U.S. Navy had commanded considerable—and, at certain points in history, absolute—authority there. In the case of a territorial dispute, the naval commodore naturally expected the FEC Railway to fall in line. Yet what the navy failed to reckon with was the power and shrewdness of a man like Henry Flagler. Flagler might have launched an open dispute with the navy over the Fleming Island dredging, or perhaps a public relations campaign, but he did not. Flagler and the FEC allowed their actions to speak for themselves. It was one thing to send away the two dredges but another to strip the Key West office bare of its furniture and light fixtures. Although the thought of eliminating the Key West terminus from his plans must have been devastating to Flagler, outwardly, his company behaved coolly. In response to War Department mandates, the plan for the Overseas Railroad seemed to have definitively changed. By the following summer, in July 1908, the FEC workforce had fallen from 2,940 to 795 men, a reduction of nearly 70 percent.[138]

In May 1908, ten months after the dredge work stopped, the *Key West Citizen* announced that "Mr. Flagler Sends Regrets to Key West." The paper told readers that "Mr. H.M. Flagler writes that his inability to visit Key West this season has caused him much regret, but he expects to make up for his loss next year by paying frequent visits to our city." One cannot help but hear a note of desperation in the next sentence: "There is no place in Florida where he will find such genuine friendship." In case there was any doubt about Key West's attitude toward the industrialist, the writer added, "We sincerely hope that his health will remain good during the summer so that he may give his great enterprise here a great deal of his time next winter." The disappointment of the community about the possibly canceled project is obvious.

For about two years, no one spotted the dredges *George Allen* or *Grampus* working off Key West's northern shore. The island city saw its hopes of connection by rail to the rest of America evaporating. To compound the bad news, Principal Assistant Engineer William Krome resigned from the project in October 1908.[139] Instead, he would oversee his groves in Homestead. The news grew even more dire when Chief Engineer Joseph Meredith died unexpectedly in April 1909.

It was quite a blow when Flagler's chosen man, Meredith, died of overwork and complications from diabetes. Fortunately, Krome agreed to come back, now as chief engineer in charge of the whole works, with his headquarters at Marathon. The railway company even presented him with a loving cup, a kind of trophy, to recognize his service. In this case, it wasn't

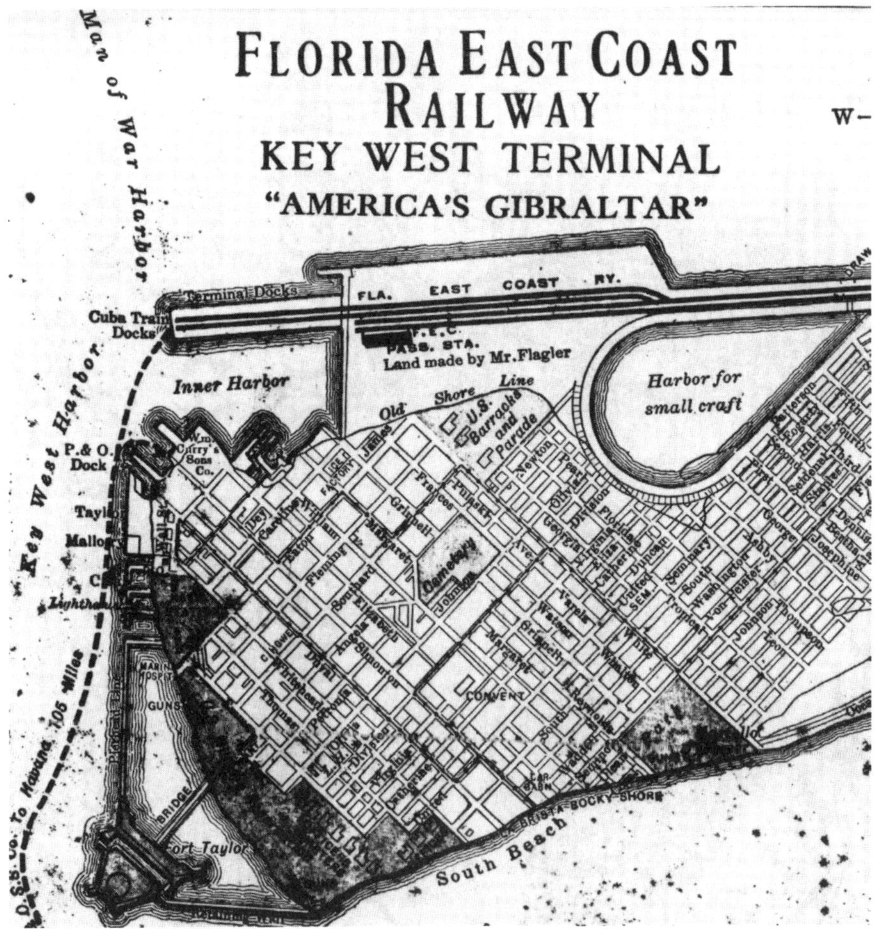

This FEC maps depicts "Land made by Mr. Flagler." *Courtesy of the Monroe County Public Library, Key West.*

for a job completed, but rather a job that still had years left to go. But would the railroad still stop in the middle of the Keys or go all the way? That was the looming question that caused so much anxiety, especially in Key West.

Then, on September 11, 1909, a newspaper announced, "Work Resumed on Trumbo Island."[140] And just like that, the public was informed that the Overseas Railroad, stretching from the Florida mainland across the scattered islands, would indeed make its way to Key West. Somehow or another, Flagler had gotten his way. The U.S. Navy raised no more objections. In fact, what should have been clear from the beginning was that the War Department needed his train system much more than the submerged fill.[141]

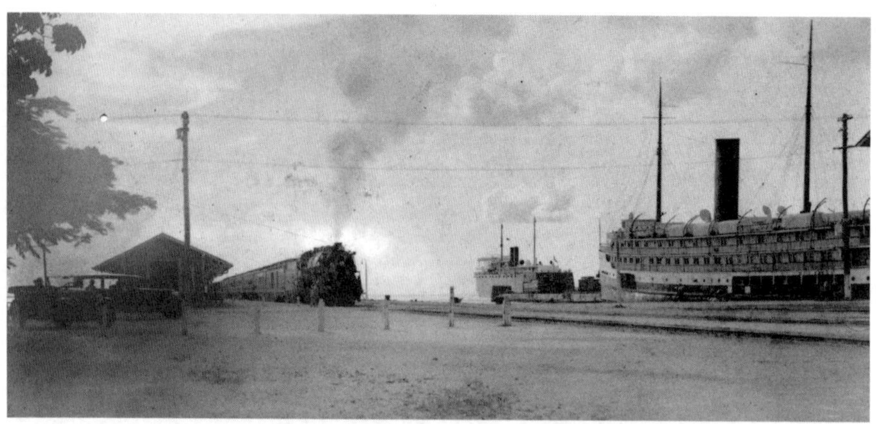

At last, the FEC station at Key West's Trumbo Point was completed. *Courtesy of the Monroe County Public Library, Key West.*

The mystery remains: what exactly happened behind the scenes? Were there feverish negotiations between the FEC and the U.S. government? Were strings pulled at the very highest levels in Washington? While the newspaper clippings in William Krome's scrapbooks tell us that the stoppage did occur and that the FEC appeared to change its goal of reaching Key West, some of this history is still hidden from view. We can surmise that some intervention took place, but how precisely the standoff was resolved in Flagler's favor still remains a mystery.

A map drawn after the railroad's completion shows the FEC's Key West terminus, along with the words "Land Made by Mr. Flagler," as though the millionaire had crafted the land with his own two hands or perhaps conjured it out of the ether like a genie. While no magic brought about the completion of the FEC's Key West Extension, one can only speculate about the particular brand of business genius that Henry Flagler used to make it happen. One final irony: years later, the U.S. Navy purchased the "Land Made by Mr. Flagler" from the FEC Railway company to use as the Trumbo Point Naval Air Station.

Chapter 6
Rumrunners and Speakeasies

The sound of a motor churning through the water was the only thing that gave the fishing boat away. Midnight had come and gone; the sole illumination emanated from a faint smattering of stars overhead and a crescent moon. The boat's running lights remained off as the rumrunner cut the engine and drifted into the leafy, waiting arms of a mangrove. He would not unload his cargo here in the Upper Keys but rather wait for a few hours, or even a day, until it seemed safe to journey onward. The only person who might dare venture into Little Snake Creek, not just at that hour but any other, would be a pal, another liquor smuggler who used the creek as a hiding hole. The rumrunners had warned revenue agents, "Leave us alone, or we'll shoot," and as a result, this particular hideout was considered off-limits to lawmen.

This scene occurred many times in Islamorada during Prohibition. Little Snake Creek had been cut off from Florida Bay by fill when Henry Flagler built his Overseas Railroad, but it stayed open on the ocean side, making it the perfect haven for rumrunners. Although the creek was not wide, it was deep, so they could bring in fairly sizeable boats. Rumrunners, including otherwise law-abiding fishermen, knew the shorelines, reefs and inlets of the various islands and where to conceal a vessel or deposit a load of "demijohns" to recover later if the Coast Guard discovered them mid-run.

Just a few years earlier, nobody had any need to "run" rum, whiskey, gin or any other spirit into the United States. But with the ratification of the Eighteenth Amendment and the passing of the Volstead Act at the end of

1919, Prohibition became a reality. Suddenly, the law mandated that "no person shall manufacture, sell, barter, transport, import, export, deliver, or furnish any intoxicating liquor." Across the Florida Keys, it was as if the residents released one long, exasperated groan in response. From the sparsely inhabited shores of Key Largo to the city streets of Key West, the majority of residents—not to mention visitors—despised this new puritanical ban on alcohol.

Because the Upper and Middle Keys saw a limited number of year-round residents in the 1920s, local law enforcement was almost nil. One lone officer made his way up and down the Keys, and somehow, the "coconut telegraph" ensured that people generally knew when he was coming. While rumrunners hid in Islamorada's Little Snake Creek (around today's mile marker 86.7, near the Montessori school), illicit watering holes catered to the thirsty on the island of Key Largo. Opened by Mabel Harris in 1928 in North Key Largo, Mabel's Place served up favorites such as Florida lobster and key lime pie, along with prohibited hooch.[142] Mabel Harris, sister of future politician Harry Harris, ran what was politely termed a "tearoom," although customers did not necessarily have any interest in a pot of Earl Grey: "In the Prohibition years, 'tearoom' was a common code name for an establishment that served alcohol."[143] Not only could customers imbibe, but they could also indulge in the services of the on-site brothel.

While Mabel's Place served patrons in North Key Largo, the Tavern Tearoom catered to clientele in Tavernier. Hugh "Mac" Mackenzie, a teacher from Dade County, arrived in the Keys in 1928 and took over the operation of the so-called tearoom (next door to the present-day Tavernier Hotel). A family man with a wife, Hazel, and daughter, Joanne, Mac oversaw the drinking and also possibly the gambling (although, unlike Mabel's, not prostitution).[144] Although enforcement of the "dry" laws occurred infrequently and sporadically, sometimes the Upper Keys did figure in the ongoing Prohibition saga. Not long before Prohibition was repealed in December 1932, a newspaper headline announced, "Colored Woman Caught on Road with Wet Goods." A certain Constable Edney Parker arrested Louise Knight in her Cadillac: "In the car was found one and a half gallons of that boon for the thirsty, who don't care what they drink, commonly called 'shine.'"[145] The unfortunate Ms. Knight was brought before the justice of the peace, E.R. Lowe, and since she apparently did not have the $200 for bail, she wound up behind bars in a Monroe County jail. In the Prohibition years, many Keys residents violated this unpopular law and sometimes paid a not insignificant price.

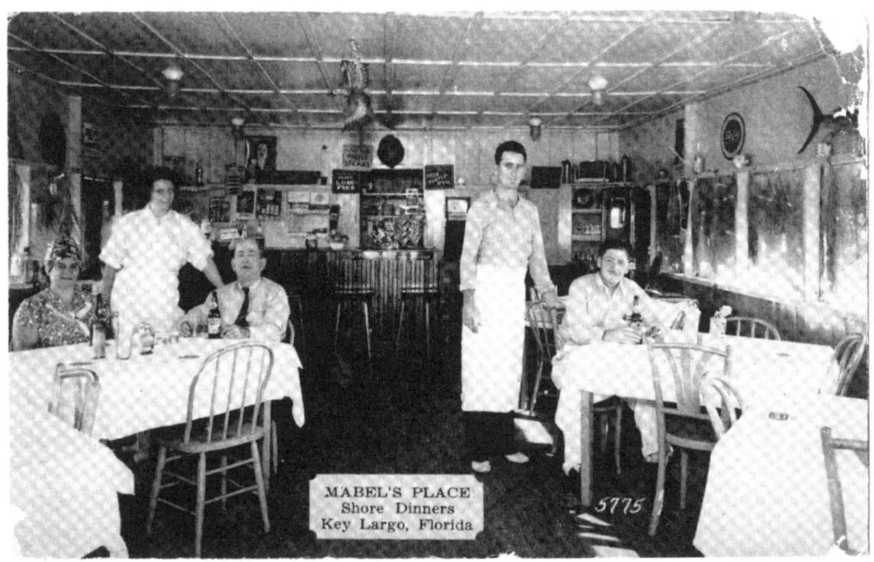

A postcard depicts Mabel's Place, which served pies, turtle steaks and, during Prohibition, liquor. *Jerry Wilkinson Collection.*

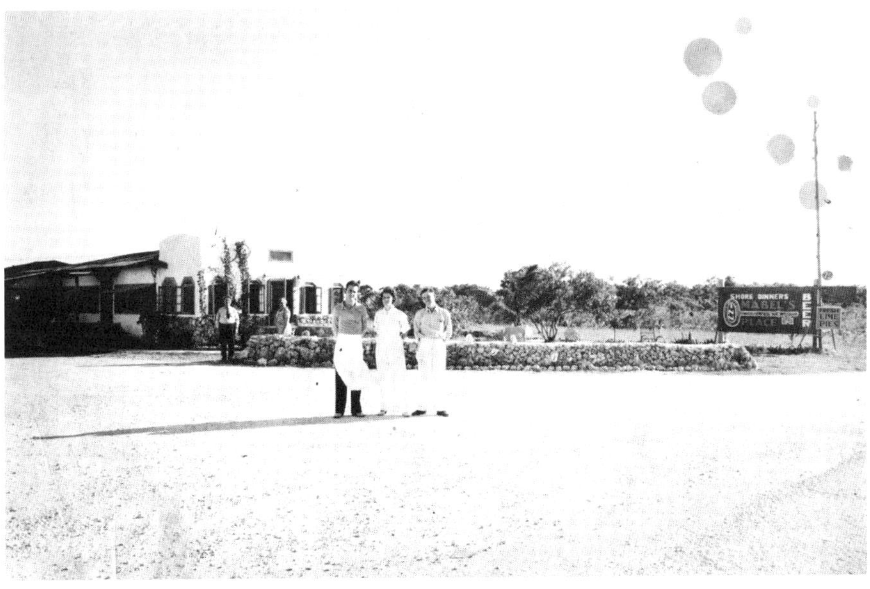

Three people pose outside Mabel's Place in North Key Largo; Mabel Harris may be in the center. *Jerry Wilkinson Collection.*

In the Upper and Middle Keys, there were only so many citizens to run afoul of Prohibition. In Key West, however, it was a truly different story. Even the island's most famous resident, Ernest Hemingway, supposedly smuggled rum in from Cuba, while his favorite fishing boat captain, Joe "Josie Grunts" Russell, operated a speakeasy on Front Street, years before opening his bar Sloppy Joe's.[146] Prior to that, Joe had allegedly sold liquor at a stand located—of all places—just outside the naval base. With Cuba and its plentiful golden rum only ninety miles away, Key West became one of America's most alcohol-drenched cities. In fact, Key West's reputation as a party town ironically has its roots in those "dry" years: one might even argue that Prohibition created Key West's hard-drinking identity.

Certainly, the reporters who accompanied President Calvin Coolidge to the island in 1928 were aware of the liquid delights that awaited. The newspapermen, including *New York Herald Tribune* journalist Beverly Smith Jr., had set out by train to document Coolidge's trip to Cuba. This necessitated a stopover in Key West before the party took a ferry to Havana. Whereas the straight-laced president supported the ban on alcohol, members of his entourage could not wait to guzzle gin, whiskey or any other outlawed liquor. After the president turned in for the evening, the journalists went on the town. "The dignity of the tour began to crack," Smith later wrote.[147] "It was as though the mice had been informed that the cat was away." A

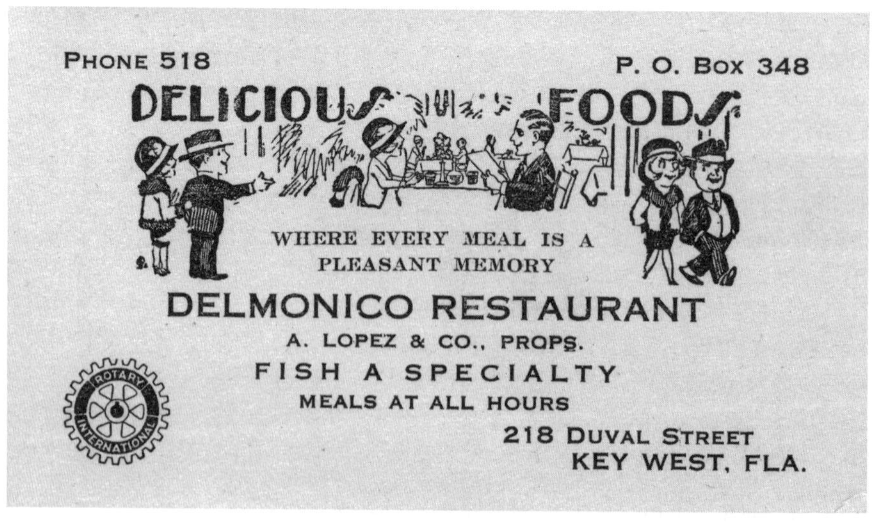

A card for Delmonico's, one of many Key West establishments that (somewhat) covertly served alcohol during Prohibition. *Courtesy of the Monroe County Public Library, Key West.*

raucous night followed at Key West night spots. Perhaps they started off at the upscale restaurant Delmonico's, which discreetly served liquor, or maybe they ventured somewhere less swish, such as a speakeasy simply described as "the place operated by Pedro Rodriguez on Emma Street."[148] Although Smith did "not remember that anybody fell down or had to be carried," he admitted that "it cannot be denied that many in our party exceeded the bounds of strict sobriety."

In films, speakeasies often appear as nightclubs hidden down mysterious alleyways, with doors where a patron would knock and give a password. In Key West, however, a speakeasy could look like any normal residence on any given street. Tampa-born Raul Vasquez lived at 1117 Duval in a two-story Conch-style house. In the early days of Prohibition, Raul opened a little bar in the back that he came to call the Florence Club. (Since a number of his patrons had married women named Florence, Raul cheekily named his spot after their long-suffering wives.[149]) There wasn't much to this speakeasy: a simple counter where drinks could be poured, a shelf to hold bottles of liquor, eight chairs for customers and also a bench. (Raul had "borrowed" the bench from Duval Street, where it had been placed at a stop for the electric streetcar.)[150] Another notable aspect of the Florence Club was a slab of white marble measuring fourteen by eighteen inches; when customers came by for a libation and found Raul out, they simply wrote down what they took—or drank on the spot—on the marble slab and paid up later. Raul recalled later that "no one ever stole a single bottle."

Given that selling liquor was illegal, even in permissive Key West, Raul could not post a sign to advertise his place of business. Some illicit watering holes did erect placards that read "Club in Rear." Instead of this route, he craftily marketed the speakeasy by way of a code carved the house's front balusters, or "gingerbread" trim. Here, in the negative space, one could make out the silhouette of bottles and also symbols for playing cards. Strangely enough, Raul did not have a Key West cabinetmaker create this bit of advertising subterfuge but rather, according to his daughter, Maria, had it crafted in his family's native Cuba.[151]

Many Key West restaurateurs and speakeasy owners relied on rumrunners to keep them regularly supplied with liquor. Raul Vasquez, on the other hand, eliminated the middle man and did the smuggling himself. Unlike some rumrunners, Raul had not previously worked on the sea as a fisherman but rather labored on land at a cigar factory, and as a result, his navigational skills were limited. Before Prohibition made a longer voyage necessary, he had only steered the small boat that he owned along the Keys

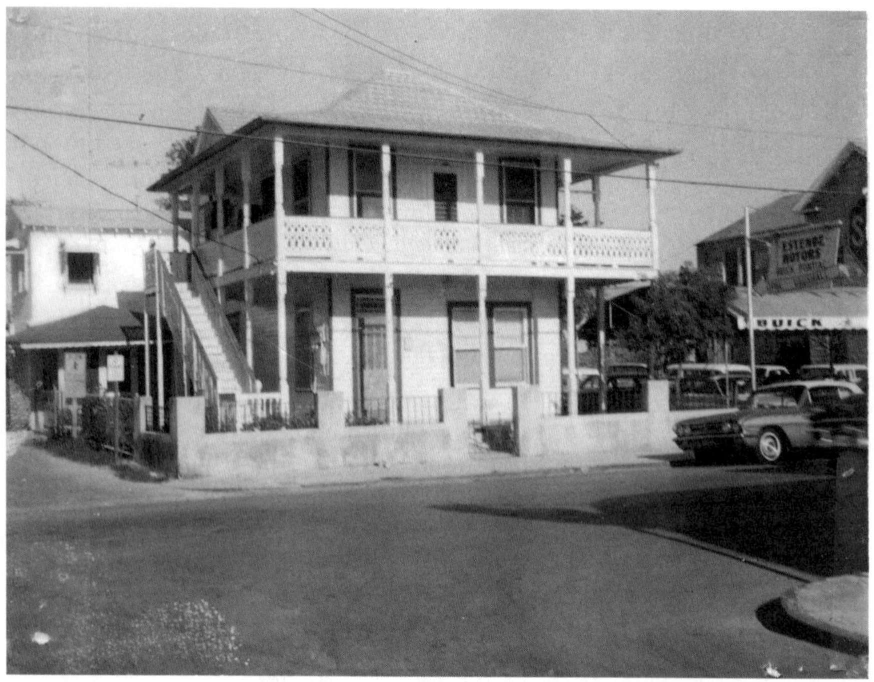

In the back of Raul Vasquez's house on Duval Street, members frequented the Florence Club. *Courtesy of the Monroe County Public Library, Key West.*

and never lost sight of land. Cruising ninety miles to Cuba presented much more of a challenge.

Before his first smuggling voyage, Raul took the precaution of purchasing a compass and asking local fishermen for advice on how to reach Havana. He hired an old salt who hung around the docks—someone like the character Eddie in the Bogart film *To Have and Have Not*—to help him with the cargo once they arrived in Cuba. Perhaps not trusting that his companion would be willing to accompany him in this small boat across the Gulf Stream, Raul did not tell him where they were headed until they had been underway for several hours.

The would-be rumrunner had calculated the trip to last about twenty-four hours, which turned out to be wildly optimistic, especially since they got lost. The compass failed to work. They might have zig-zagged, directionless, at sea and eventually run out of gas, but Raul managed to find a way to steer by the stars. After a few harrowing days, they arrived in Cuba—and then spent additional days making their way to Havana. There Raul and his single crewman met with a dealer and loaded the bottles of alcohol on board. Apparently, the man selling them the liquor "thought that Raul's boat was merely a dinghy and that he was going to transfer his cargo to a larger boat outside the harbor."[152]

Although Raul spoke with more experienced sailors before setting out from Havana for Key West, the return trip presented its own set of challenges. First, the little boat's engine gave them trouble, and then the sea frothed with turbulent waves. The cargo, too heavy for such a small craft, weighed it down so much that both men feared they might sink. Yet Raul stubbornly refused to toss any of the bottles overboard. Finally, and almost miraculously, he recognized the tree-lined shores of Big Pine Key in the distance. Despite being blown off course and nearly capsizing, they had reached the safety of land.

After that first chaotic trip, Raul Vasquez became a practiced and highly successful rumrunner. At one point, he supplied a Shriners' convention in Key West with an incredible 150 suitcases of alcohol.[153] He also supplied hooch to salesmen who hawked real estate during the Florida Land Boom; apparently, offering potential buyers a little tipple helped to move deals along. As Key West grew in importance in the South Florida rum smuggling racket, the Coast Guard expanded its presence there and put increasing pressure on Keys rumrunners. Given the number of runs he completed, it was almost inevitable that Raul Vasquez would be arrested and land in jail.

Raul had always had a trustworthy reputation locally, and that, coupled with Key West's general disdain for Prohibition, ensured that his jail time was anything but oppressive. The jailers understood that Raul, a businessman, had business to attend to and therefore allowed him to leave the jail during the day, accomplish his tasks and return at night. Sometimes these tasks included overseeing the arrival of a new shipment of liquor! On a few occasions when Raul's activities made him late, he found the jail entrance locked. Then he would bang and bang until the jailer awoke and let him back in. Finally, the jailer simply gave Raul a key, so that he didn't wake him.[154] As they say, only in Key West. Unlike many involved in the illicit booze trade who were shot or drowned at sea, Raul's extraordinary luck held, and after Prohibition, he opened a legitimate establishment on East Roosevelt Boulevard called Raul's Club, where sharks and parrotfish entertained visitors both old and young.

Raul Vasquez was hardly the only rumrunner in the Florida Keys who had trouble with the authorities. Despite the lukewarm enforcement, Prohibition remained the law until 1933, and both local law officers and visiting "Revenuers," or IRS agents, did crack down from time to time. In September 1932, for instance, two customs officers, O.C. Lounders and L.C. Taylor, found themselves driving in pursuit of a smuggler in Key West. The

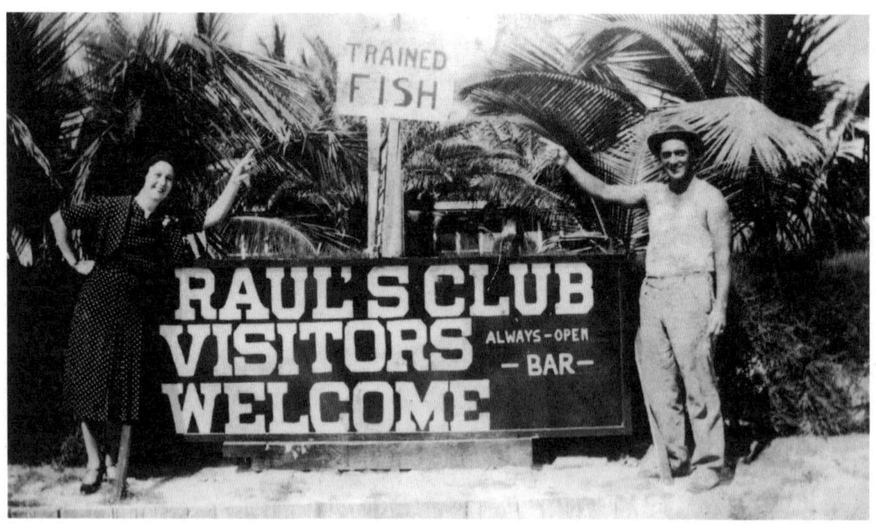

Raul Vasquez, former rumrunner and speakeasy operator, posing at his legitimate establishment after Prohibition ended. *Courtesy of the Monroe County Public Library, Key West.*

Key West Citizen reported, "When the driver of the car found that capture was inevitable he left the car and started running for safety. So precipitate was his flight that he left his engine running." On that particular day, the officers hauled in "twelve 5 gallon demijohns of Bacardi, two 1 gallon demijohns of the same elixir and two quarts of compuesta, not to mention a Chevrolet coach."[155] Often, when the newspaper reported on "busts," the news could only be found buried, pages in, among other local notices and updates. However, one bust found its way onto the front page, with the headline "Customs Officials of This City Make Rich Bacardi Haul."

At that time, decades before the Cuban Revolution, the Bacardi family still manufactured their rum in Cuba. As rums went, Bacardi ranked among the best-known, and certainly Key West's rumrunners showed good taste in spirits when they tried to illegally import no fewer than 196 gallons of Bacardi. Unfortunately for the smugglers, on February 17, 1927, customs officials caught up with them on Stock Island. They arrested Justo Larto, the man driving the first getaway car (a Ford coupe), but the driver of the second (a Cole Eight) made his escape.[156] Customs officer L.C. Taylor also figured in this capture, along with his colleagues A.G. Lund, Charles S. Williams and Charles M. Russell. Rumrunning must have been incredibly profitable, because the customs men noted that "the car seized last night belongs to a party who has already lost five automobiles in this same way."[157] Given the expense of a car in the 1920s, the fact that the smuggling kingpin (or queenpin) could afford these losses speaks volumes.

Not all raids ended with the lawmen covered in glory. In April 1927, ten prohibition officers from Lake Worth, led by Deputy Prohibition Administrator W.M. Simmons, descended on Key West. They must have known the island's reputation as a veritable mecca for drink, and the "prohis," as they were called, were eager to nab some criminals. Despite "a score and more" raids (well over twenty), in the end, they could drum up charges against a mere six men. One can only conjecture that in this instance, Key Westers protected their own. As one old-timer remarked to a *Key West Citizen* reporter, "They come down here and bagged a lot of minners and all the big ones got away."[158]

One big fish who got away was interviewed by Florida folklorist Stetson Kennedy in 1938, five years after the end of Prohibition. Even with alcohol then legal in the United States, this charter boat captain turned rumrunner from Key West still preferred to use a pseudonym, "Captain Antonio," when speaking of his past. He and a comrade known to us only as "Garcia" regularly brought in Scotch, rye, gin, rum, Champagne and wine from Cuba. The smuggler noted that "Key West was one of the few towns in the country where you could get stuff that wasn't watered."[159] The high quality of Key West's liquor supply made it even more alluring for those in search of a drink. The risks of rumrunning, however, meant that it could be difficult for speakeasy owners and restauranteurs to keep a good supply of booze on hand and thus keep their customers happy. "Me and Garcia had a good reputation—could practically guarantee delivery. That gave us good business. We always went around and got up orders and collected in advance before we made a trip."

Although they could make fabulous profits, rumrunning involved real danger and was an anxiety-producing line of work. After taking orders from their clients, Captain Antonio and Garcia set out for Cuba:

> [T]*hat Gulf Stream gets might rough for small boats. I've crossed the channel in a storm with only a coupla inches freeboard. We moved at night. Sometimes the customs pushed us so close we had to drop the load overboard. Then all they could hold us for was running without lights. When they would get on our tail we'd make a run for shallow water where we could lose em, or at least drop the load and picks it up later on. Used to hate to have to throw stuff over in deep water. A good friend of mine drowned tryn to save a few extra bottles.*[160]

One of the biggest hazards to any rumrunner did not stem from law enforcement but rather fellow lawbreakers, as Captain Antonio explained. "The damned pelicans…bothered us more than customs. Them pelicans knew the water good as we did. We never knew when they was watchin us hide a load under water. That's why we call em pelicans—they'd wait till we was gone, and then they'd dive down and bring up the load."[161] The opportunists whom the smugglers called "pelicans" did not make the liquor runs to Cuba or the Bahamas themselves; they stole from rumrunners who had hidden a shipment or ditched a load in shallow water.

One day, Captain Antonio and Garcia had a ship-full of booze, but a customs boat had arrived in Key West. Rather than risk being discovered landing their cargo in the harbor, the two men secreted the bottles nearby on Cow Key (off Stock Island), among some tall grasses. While Garcia drove their boat back to Key West, the captain stayed on Cow Key to keep an eye on their valuable contraband. He noticed that

> *the next day a coupla strange fishermen landed to cook lunch. I give em a few keys of wine to keep quiet. It turned out that the odd fishermen weren't really fishermen at all, but undercover agents. They hadn't been gone long when the customs boat swung out of Key West and headed straight for me. I didn't have no boat, so I just waited for em to land.… You know what happened? The customs marshall got me to slip the whole load into his garage.*[162]

Native Conch Paul "Deacon" Lowe started rumrunning out of Key West when he was just nineteen. Soon he was making regular trips to Havana, Nassau and Bimini with two other men to procure four hundred cases and one hundred hooch-filled demijohns. The demand for liquor seemed insatiable. "If we could've run down there everyday we couldn't have brought back enough stuff to supply everybody," he said.[163] Like Raul Vasquez, he had multiple encounters with the law. Finally, a Coast Guard cutter successfully intercepted him and attached a tow line to Deacon's vessel. In a desperate rush to escape, he poured liquor all over his boat and set it on fire. As the flames leaped higher, he jumped into the sea. The Coast Guard managed to retrieve him. Yet when Deacon went before a sympathetic judge for sentencing, he received only one month in Miami jail.[164] Some rumrunners he knew were not so fortunate. "There were a lot of us in the business but most of them didn't live to see the end of prohibition," Deacon told a reporter years later.[165]

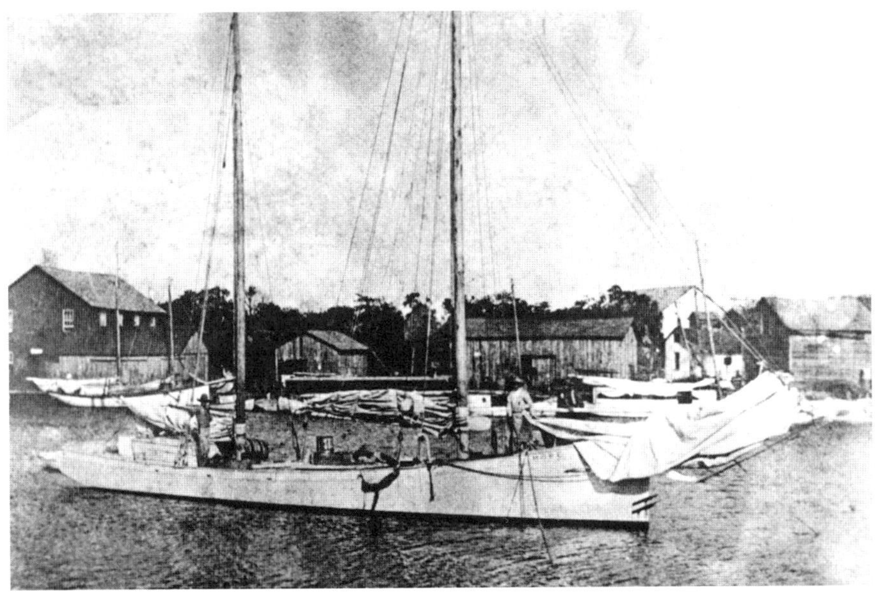

This sailing vessel, *Island Home*, ran rum throughout the Florida Keys. *Courtesy of the State Archives of Florida.*

Captain Antonio also personally knew smugglers whose luck ran out. One notorious rumrunner, nicknamed "Cockeye Billy,"

> *could swim like a fish, and that's how he made a lot of his getaways. He'd high-ball for shallow water, snake through the channels, and head up into some mangrove swamp. In some of these creeks we had pockets cut outen the mangroves and he would run his boat into the pocket and pull down the mangroves behind him. He even cut pieces to scatter over the top of the boat to keep the customs airplanes from spottin it in the daytime.*[166]

The smuggler known as Cockeye Billy impressed even other rumrunners with his ability to elude the law: "If they cornered Cockeye he'd dive overboard, swim under water, and come up way back in the swamp. He was just like a fish in the water." Then, one evening, about two miles from the closest island, customs agents caught up with him. Bullets flew both ways, and Cockeye went over the side of his boat. He never resurfaced. "Nobody senn him since," his friend Captain Antonio revealed sadly. "The government men saw blood on his boat and reported he'd got drowned or the sharks had got him."[167] Still, his legendary abilities under water made some of his comrades reluctant to give up hope. "Ever now and then some of the boys up on the Keys gits drunk and say they seen Cockeye in Tampa or Miami," the captain remarked. "But he wasn't that good a swimmer."[168]

One of the most legendary and ruthless rumrunners to bring liquor from Cuba to Key West—and points beyond—was a woman. "Spanish Marie," they called her, although her real name was Marie Waite. Standing nearly six feet tall, with lush black hair and magnetic blue eyes, she headquartered her smuggling empire in Havana, beyond the reach of American lawmen. Not actually Spanish at all, Marie Waite had Swedish and Mexican parentage.[169] Sources claim that this Amazon was "an astute business woman of iron determination" with "morals as free as the four winds."[170] Marie had been married to Charlie Waite, a "Miami liquor runner who disappeared following an encounter with coast guards in the waters south of Miami in 1926."[171] With her husband dead and their children to support, Marie took over her husband's operation; she used her smarts and strategic sense to import huge quantities of illicit alcohol from both Cuba and the Bahamas to the Florida Keys, as well as South Florida.

Operating in a tough, male-dominated world, Spanish Marie thrived. It was hardly an easy time to make one's mark as a female entrepreneur. American women had only won the right to vote in 1920, and much of society still believed that a woman's place was in the home. Yet social conventions meant nothing to Marie Waite. She took a string of lovers, most of whom were fellow rumrunners. She would gladly bribe officials to overlook her crimes. Over time, Spanish Marie acquired fifteen speedboats "which she controlled and directed, all of which were capable of 20 to 30 knots."[172]

The Coast Guard, responsible for the death of her husband, Charlie, became her enemy, and outwitting or outrunning its patrols became her primary aim. Often, her boats traveled in convoys of four, with three of the vessels carrying liquor and a fourth with no liquor but "armed to the teeth."[173] If they came under fire, the fourth boat could take on the Coast Guard cutter while the other three vessels slipped away. When the Coast Guard attempted to clamp down on her smuggling flotillas, Marie had radios installed on her boats and then opened "an unlicensed radio transmitting station at Key West for communication with them." The code she created to keep their smuggling crossings secret consisted of "seemingly harmless Spanish words and phrases."[174] Unfortunately for her, lawmen eventually discovered the Key West station, and her code was broken.

In 1931, Spanish Marie (by then Marie Waite Saez, having remarried, this time to a Cuban) found herself arrested after leaving Havana for Florida. The arrest was connected to a smuggling ring that extended from Florida to New Orleans and a boat called the *Coca Cola Kid*, which had been discovered with \$150,000 worth of liquor on board (about \$2.5 million today, accounting for inflation).[175] A judge set bail at \$15,000, a huge amount of money in that era, which Marie nonetheless paid.[176] At this point, Spanish Marie seems to have disappeared from newspapers and the public record. She left behind no photographs, or at least none that we have been able to locate—only her remarkable record as one of the most prolific rumrunners ever to operate in the Florida Keys.

In the waning months of Prohibition, the *Key West Citizen* ran articles about the debate between the "wets" and the "drys" on the front page. On one hand, the Florida Keys were ready to see alcohol legalized, while on the other, the end of the Prohibition period would signal an end to the enormous profits that many rumrunners and speakeasy operators in the Keys had enjoyed. By 1933, when Prohibition was at last repealed, American had slid into the Great Depression. The Florida Keys felt this financial pain acutely; unemployment became overwhelming. Key West itself slid into bankruptcy, and many Conchs survived on a monotonous diet of fish and hominy grits. As Prohibition ended and legitimate bars opened their doors once again on Duval Street and beyond, the surviving rumrunners returned to a more mundane existence. Soon those wild, dangerous years of ill-gotten riches and bootlegged booze faded to a hazy memory.

Chapter 7
Swells Descend on the Upper Keys

Photographs of pioneers who settled among the Upper Keys in the late nineteenth and early twentieth centuries show a determined, hardy people. The women look composed and proper in corsets and long dresses despite the tropical heat, while their husbands stare soberly into the camera. Only children's expressions sometimes hint at mischief and freewheeling exuberance. For the most part, life on the twenty-seven-mile-long island of Key Largo and among the scattered isles of Islamorada was hard. Families supported themselves by fishing and farming crops such as grapefruit and pineapples; even little ones helped their parents with difficult chores. Pioneering families needed to be self-reliant, although they could sail north to buy goods in Miami and Coconut Grove, which as of the 1890s, were very small but growing communities.

Around the turn of the century in North Key Largo, a fishing camp and trading post sprang up on the bay side of the island.[177] The property quietly passed through different hands, including those of W.A. Scott of Fargo, North Dakota, who in 1912, no doubt seeking a congenial place to winter, built himself a handsome, two-story home of coral rock.[178] Mr. Scott sold to a Mr. Stranahan, and so things might have continued, unremarkably, on this obscure acreage in the Upper Keys where the camp attracted a small number of fishermen.

Still sparsely inhabited, the Upper Keys were hardly a destination for holidaymakers. In fact, all of the Florida Keys, including Key West, were latecomers to the tourism racket, and even the opening of the Overseas

Railroad in 1912 did not boost tourism as expected. In the 1920s, swanky hotels Casa Marina and La Concha opened in Key West, yet tourism still had a modest financial impact on the island. Meanwhile, during the feverish Florida Land Boom in the 1920s, developers bought up Upper Keys land and sold off plots in speculative developments with names like Palma Sola and Largo Beach.[179] One developer even built a post office, a restaurant and a little hotel beside the Key Largo train depot,[180] but still, few people trickled into the Upper Florida Keys to holiday. Two factors would change this state of things: the growing appetite in America for warm, seaside vacations and the opening of a new route south.

In 1928, the first motorists eagerly sped south from mainland Florida across the new Card Sound Road and onto the island of Key Largo. (To reach Key West, motorists had to use a combination of roads and car ferries.) Suddenly, the Florida Keys were accessible to Americans who preferred to travel by automobile, rather than be limited by a train timetable.

After the first Overseas Highway opened, the simple fishing camp at North Key Largo was acquired by Henry L. Doherty. Founder of an oil conglomerate and "one of the richest men in America,"[181] Doherty had discovered the allure of South Florida and decided to invest. He bailed out the failing Biltmore Hotel in Coral Gables and then bought the Plaza Hotel on Miami Beach.[182] (With the Florida Land Boom bubble decisively deflated, several properties were struggling.) In the early 1930s, Colonel Doherty turned his sights to the quiet anglers' camp, which was ripe for reinvention. Doherty's Roney Investment Company would import vacationers to rough it, but in a certain style. The new and improved "Florida Year-Round Club" would be all about exclusivity.[183]

Local pioneers whose simple, wood-frame homes had no electricity must have been flabbergasted to see the "swells" descend on their island. The settlers' Spartan way of life stood in contrast to the luxuries and technologies enjoyed by upscale city-dwellers who ventured to North Key Largo for an island escape. Certain visitors arrived from Coral Gables on the club-owned speedboat that Doherty nicknamed the "Sea Sled."[184] Still others rode from Miami on "Aerocars," a semi-trailer kind of bus.[185] The most elite of all were flown in on the club's Auto-Gyro, a newfangled airplane-helicopter hybrid. For some Upper Keys children, the Auto-Gyro might have been their first glimpse of an airplane.

Chic women and men began arriving regularly to stay in the club's comfortably furnished cottages. Wait staff, housekeeping staff and fishing guides ensured that guests felt amply catered to. Visitors enjoyed delicious

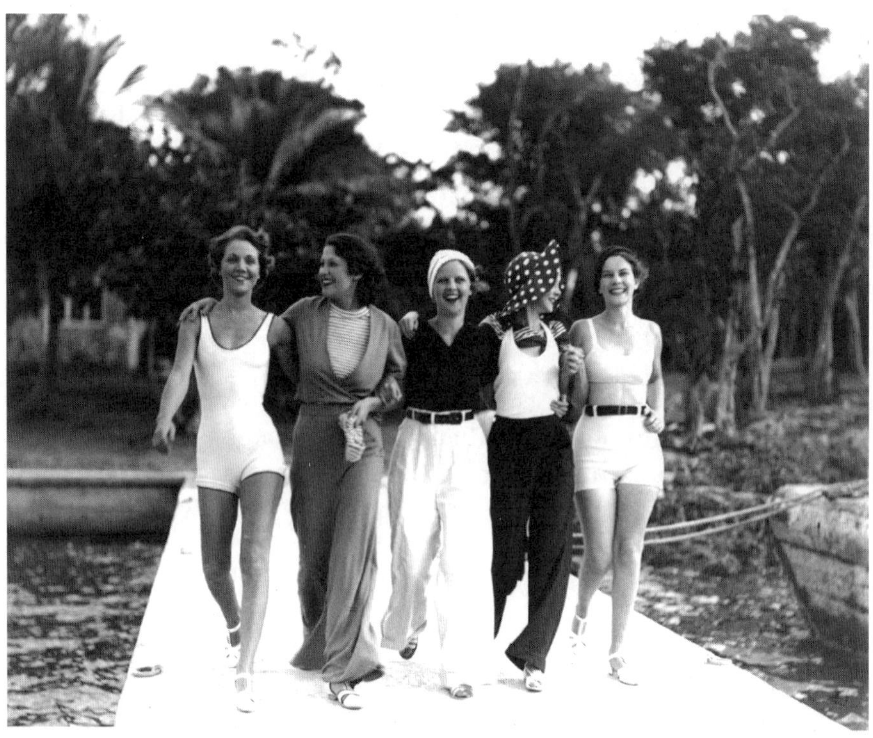

Young women at the Key Largo Angler's Club in 1932. *Courtesy of the Monroe County Public Library, Key West.*

meals at dinnertime, under twinkling lights powered by the club's generators. Without being pretentious, the now renamed Key Largo Angler's Club offered the experience of a well-run, discreetly located resort on the waterfront.

Despite the glitz of the Auto-Gyro and Aerocars, the Key Largo Angler's Club was a world away from flashy see-and-be-seen resorts at Miami or Palm Beach. People did not travel to North Key Largo to "be seen"—they came to be invisible. Two of the more famous personalities that "disappeared" at the club arrived in February 1934. Crime writer Dashiell Hammett and playwright Lillian Hellman wanted to escape freezing New York weather and the pressures of their careers. Dashiell's success was galloping along, with his book *The Thin Man* seeing good sales; MGM buying the movie rights gave the author a major cash windfall. (Lillian Hellman's own celebrity emerged later, with the success of such plays as *The Little Foxes* and *Watch on the Rhine*.)

To their fellow anglers, Dashiell and Lillian must have seemed like *The Thin Man*'s sophisticated, crime-solving couple, Nick and Nora Charles, with their witty repartee and enthusiastic drinking, save for one detail: they weren't married. Dashiell wrote regularly to his wife, Josephine, or "Jose," although their marriage was at that point in name only. In corresponding with her from North Key Largo, he naturally omitted any mention of his traveling companion, Lillian, when he explained, "There is absolutely nothing to do here but fish and swim and eat."[186] He remarked that the lights turned off at half past ten o'clock (which indicates the hour the Angler's Club shut down its generators). In a letter to his daughters, he described the coconut palm trees and how he attempted to catch a sailfish. He wrote, "All I caught was a grouper (a fat ugly fish that looks something like a catfish)" and barracuda, "with great big teeth like dogs," which "are supposed to be more dangerous than sharks."[187] He urged the girls to report to their mother than he turned in at 10:00 p.m. and woke at 6:00 a.m. Again, he would hardly tell his daughters about the woman who had supplanted their mother in his affections. Instead, he added, in language that reflects the era, that he was "as sunburned as a Zulu, and am feeling better than I have felt for years."[188]

The brilliant couple relaxed in Key Largo for weeks as they swam, ventured out on fishing expeditions and read books at their leisure.[189] In the 1930s, Dashiell Hammett was enough of a literary celebrity that the cottage where he and Lillian Hellman stayed became known as the "Dashiell Hammett Cottage."[190] The fact that a famous writer had lodged at the club added a certain cachet, and the cottage kept the name until an even more famous individual spent the night.

Former president Herbert Hoover loved to fish in the Florida Keys; he had been known to visit Henry Flagler's Long Key Fishing Camp and Thompson's Docks in Marathon.[191] In the late 1940s or thereabouts, the president arrived at the Key Largo Angler's Club and took a liking to what he saw. Local fishing guides Slim Pinder and Calvin Albury accompanied Hoover on expeditions that he thoroughly enjoyed. In 1950, an artist painted a portrait of the former president with guide Calvin Albury in a small boat. In the picture, Hoover wears a suit and tie, which indeed was how he dressed—even while fishing. That painting would eventually hang on the wall of the club's dining room, in the same coral rock house that W.A. Scott built in 1912.[192] Not only did the club make the former president an honorary commodore, but people also began calling the Dashiell Hammett Cottage the "Hoover Cottage."

Like its neighbor the Ocean Reef Club, the Key Largo Angler's Club has endured over the decades. It survived changes in ownership as well as

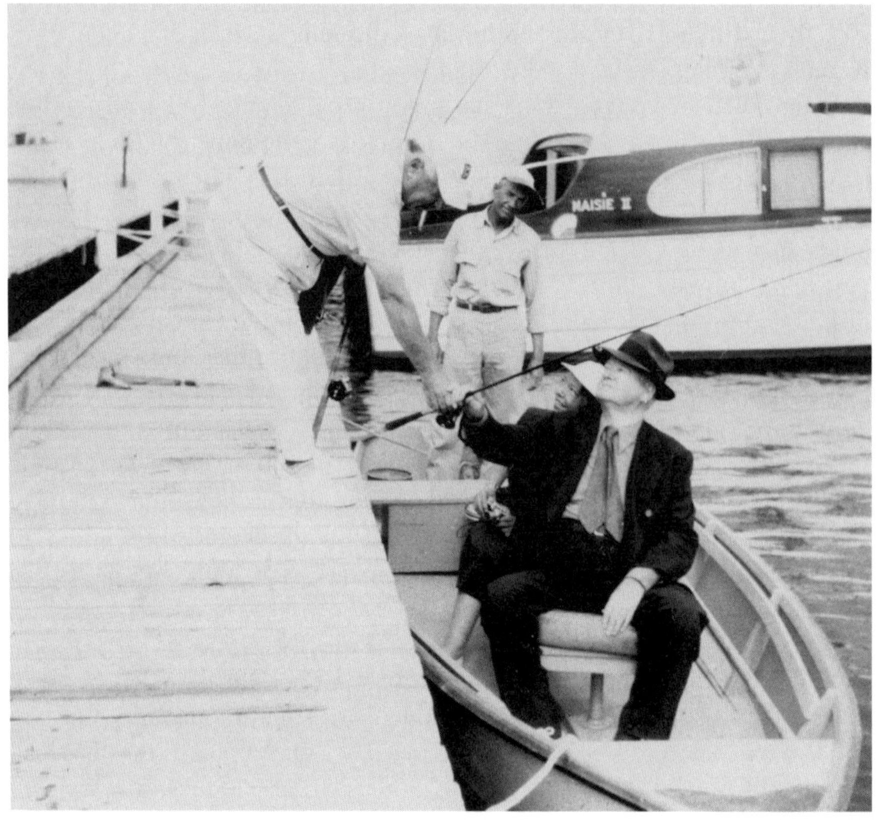

President Hoover became a regular guest at the Key Largo Angler's Club. *Courtesy of the Monroe County Public Library, Key West.*

hurricanes, including a direct hit by Hurricane Betsy in 1965. Sadly, not all Upper Keys fishing camps can claim such a long and successful run.

Coral Gables developer and early Miami pioneer George Merrick needed redemption after a catastrophic financial failure. Although he had founded an elaborate town, Coral Gables (modeled on cities in Italy and Spain); built up the University of Miami; and supervised the development of parks, plazas, neighborhoods and even a glamorous "Venetian Pool," the year 1930 saw him essentially bankrupt and broke. His real estate dreams, once covered by national newspapers, had been shattered, due in part to the crash of the Florida Land Boom, in part to the onset of the Great Depression and in part because George Merrick's ambitions simply outstretched certain financial realities. But there were twenty acres in the Florida Keys on Upper Matecumbe where he still might create something magnificent.[193]

The land was not exactly George's to develop: he had purchased the property for his wife Eunice's parents, Alfred Peacock and Lillian Frow Peacock, ten years before, back when George was flush with cash.[194] (His wife's family were also early South Florida settlers.) Now that his father-in-law was dead, George Merrick asked mother-in-law Lillian if he might take over this land for a new project.[195] She readily agreed. This became George's last chance to make a real estate comeback, and thus the Caribbee Colony was born.

Initially, the thought was simply to build a high-class fishing camp in Islamorada. But then the plan grew more complicated. George Merrick being George Merrick, a single resort or marina would not have been nearly impressive enough. He proposed to replicate the Caribbee Colony (once constructed) at ten additional locations, from Cuba to the Bahamas.[196] First, however, he needed to complete the compound on Upper Matecumbe. With the help of an architect and construction workers, soon white cabins with green trim and Samoan-style thatch huts rose up next on the shore. Well-heeled guests could stay overnight; others who were not quite as well-to-do were encouraged to join a "Caribbee Caravan" from Miami (with gas paid for by the Caribbee Colony) for day tours. Visitors could also make the trip on an FEC train reserved for Caribbee guests. For one small price, day visitors could swim, fish, dine and dance.[197] Presumably, they could

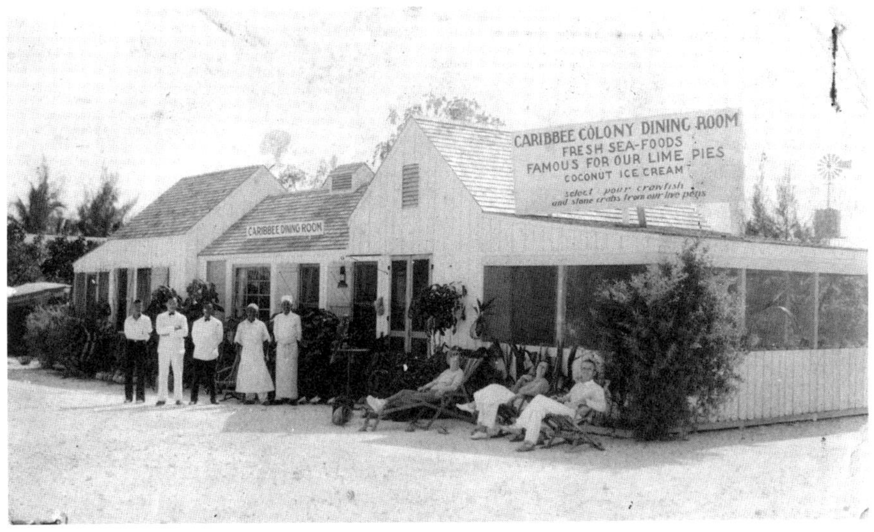

Guests and staff outside the Caribbee Colony's restaurant in the early 1930s. *Courtesy of the Monroe County Public Library, Key West.*

also imbibe a cocktail or two, despite Prohibition. Although the apparent goal was to establish a beachfront resort, in the back of George Merrick's mind was ultimately a different scheme: to entice these daytrippers to invest in property.

In December 1930 and January 1931, the Caribbee Colony on Islamorada attracted positive press, and business started to pick up. Yet bad luck seemed to dog George Merrick, as "a fire destroyed many of the huts and cabins and forced its closure."[198] Although repairs were made and some rebuilding done, the setback severely discouraged the developer. Instead of running the operation himself, George allowed a couple, Wayne and Nicky Dumas, to lease Caribbee Colony for $120 per month and run it themselves.[199] It may not have been the great empire of resorts that George had envisioned, but guests came, and the lease brought in a bit of income for the Merricks.

Despite the lean years of the Depression, enough "swells" turned up from 1931 through 1935 to turn the Caribbee Colony, under the Dumases' supervision, into a going concern. Archival photographs of the place show African American butlers and wait staff in crisp white jackets, while smiling white guests lounge back in their folding chairs as if they had discovered a carefree paradise. Here was a refuge from not only harsh winters up north but also the cares and worries of a sputtering American economy.

As anyone who knows Florida Keys history will realize, however, Islamorada was not an auspicious place to be as Labor Day dawned in 1935. Warnings had reached the Upper Keys of an incoming hurricane, yet only a limited number of people evacuated. Meteorology was in an embryonic stage, and residents did not understand the magnitude of what would come. In the final hours before the storm hit, men working to construct the Overseas Highway, mostly war veterans, were told that a train would arrive from the mainland to shepherd them to safety. George Merrick's wife, Eunice, and her mother, Lillian, had considered spending Labor Day at the Caribbee Colony but decided against it.[200] That decision almost certainly saved their lives.

Innkeepers Wayne and Nicky Dumas and their twenty-four vacationers were not so fortunate. As the hurricane approached, the storm battered Islamorada with nearly two-hundred-mile-per-hour winds. A hugely powerful storm surge swept people, animals, trees and houses clean away. The train that had been meant to rescue railroad workers was blown off its tracks; 485 souls perished in the storm.[201] The Great Labor Day Hurricane of 1935 was one of the worst natural disasters ever to hit Florida.

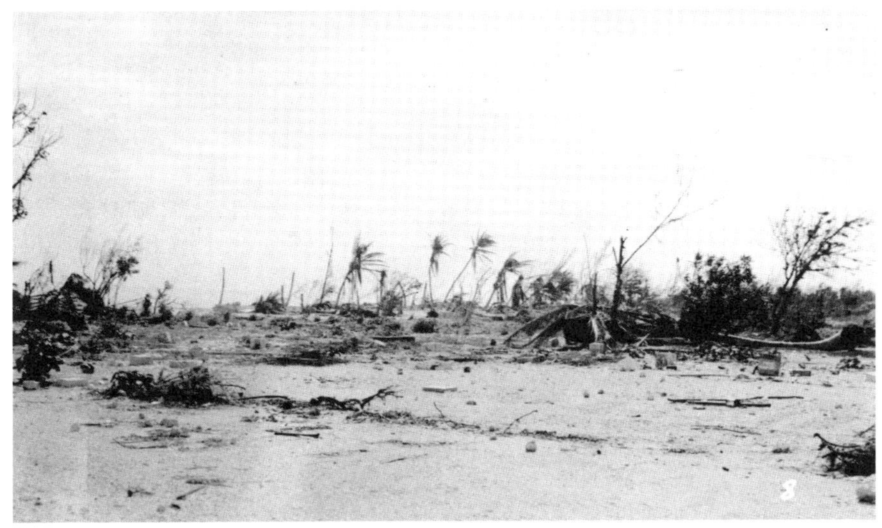

The Labor Day hurricane of 1935 obliterated the Caribbee Colony resort. *Courtesy of the Monroe County Public Library, Key West.*

The Caribbee Colony had been effectively erased from the earth—only broken palm trees remained where the resort once stood. After the storm, George Merrick journeyed down from Miami to his island property. To his credit, he went with the initial emergency responders and even assisted in carrying corpses onto a train so that they could be interred in Miami.[202] The horror of the scene traumatized almost everyone who arrived in the aftermath.

The Caribbee Colony was no more, and with its erasure died George's hopes to reemerge as an important developer. The family still owned the land, but there were no more plans to lure the swell crowd down to Islamorada for a sun-filled holiday. As Islamorada slowly rebuilt, other men and women would import their own dreams of resorts and marinas that might attract travelers to these still relatively obscure islands. World War II temporarily put a halt to this activity, although one wartime development would make establishing a business in the Florida Keys much easier: the navy helped fund a pipeline that brought fresh water to the Keys. In the postwar boom, with the Depression now a memory, tourism finally exploded. The Upper Keys became a desirable getaway for fishermen and sun worshippers, but George Merrick, who died in 1942 at the age of fifty-five, would not live to see the "beautiful people" return.

Chapter 8

The Other Treasure Hunters

The hunt for treasure—silver bars, earrings dripping with priceless emeralds—has lured men and women to the Florida Reef for hundreds of years. In the colonial era, when ships sailed from the New World to the Old, they were often laden with incredible cargoes destined to bankroll the empires of Europe. Hundreds of Spanish galleons leaving from Cartagena, Vera Cruz and Havana sailed past the Florida Keys, which they called Los Martires, the Martyrs. More than a few Spaniards were martyred here, as their ships skirted the islands and encountered the Florida Reef. Today, the Florida Reef seems like a paradise, where scores of tropical fish flash by and purple sea fans gently undulate in the currents. But hundreds of years ago, these same sharp, uncharted corals represented extreme danger and, in some cases, death for passengers on their way back to Spain (or, in other cases, England or the northern coast of the United States). As the ships foundered, broke apart and descended to the depths, they carried their precious cargoes with them.

Even centuries ago, when diving equipment was primitive or nonexistent, people could not resist the temptation to retrieve the pieces of eight and golden chalices that had been carried to the sea floor as a ship sank. In some cases, Indians were recruited and managed to free dive and bring treasures back to the surface. It was very dangerous work recovering gold and silver that the ocean had swallowed.

Despite these early salvage efforts, shipwrecks still lay scattered throughout the reef off the Florida Keys. One man who became captivated by the romance and potential riches of treasure hunting was, of course, Mel Fisher. With his distinctive eyeglasses, broad grin and persistent optimism ("Today's the day!"), Fisher spent sixteen years with his family and crew hunting for the remains of Nuestra Señora de Atocha. After finally locating $450 million worth of gold, silver and other artifacts, he became internationally famous. Books, newspaper articles and films celebrated his accomplishments and also recorded the family tragedies that the Fishers endured. Today, the Mel Fisher Maritime Heritage Museum in Key West showcases some of his accomplishments. Although Fisher passed away in 1998, mention the words "treasure hunter" and "the Florida Keys" in one sentence and one certainly cannot help but think of him.

Before Fisher's tremendous discovery and widespread fame, however, others searched the waters off the Florida Keys for treasure. Some were enthusiastic amateurs, while others were professionals. These twentieth-century adventurers have largely been forgotten by the general public (although the History of Diving Museum in Islamorada preserves much of this history). Although these treasure hunters did not find hundreds of millions of dollars worth of gold, they did help pioneer treasure hunting in the Keys and, in some cases, developed methods and technology that would make the search more feasible.

Bill Thompson fell in love with the Middle Keys in the late 1930s when he arrived for a fishing trip and discovered a largely undeveloped, sparsely inhabited island wonderland. While out at the Delta Shoal, south of Boot Key, Bill spotted ancient cannons "piled like matchsticks" on the ocean floor.[203] He would not forget the sight of those artifacts, even years after the vacation. In 1941, Bill and Ethel Thompson decided to make their home in Marathon, despite it being a sleepy little place without a reliable source of fresh water or electricity.[204] He and Ethel invested in a waterfront property and soon developed Marathon's first yacht basin, initially named the fairly no-nonsense Marathon Yacht Basin and, later, the more personal Thompson's Docks. Then World War II interrupted their plans for expansion.

During World War II, salvagers in the Florida Keys brought up a number of cannons from wreck sites, including on the Delta Shoal, and sold them as scrap metal for the war effort. At the time, there was no real appreciation of these objects as important archaeological finds. But that would change after the war.

When Bill Thompson returned from serving in the Pacific, he and Ethel once again began to build up their Marathon resort and marina. He took his boat out once again to the Delta Shoal, where he spotted two cannons

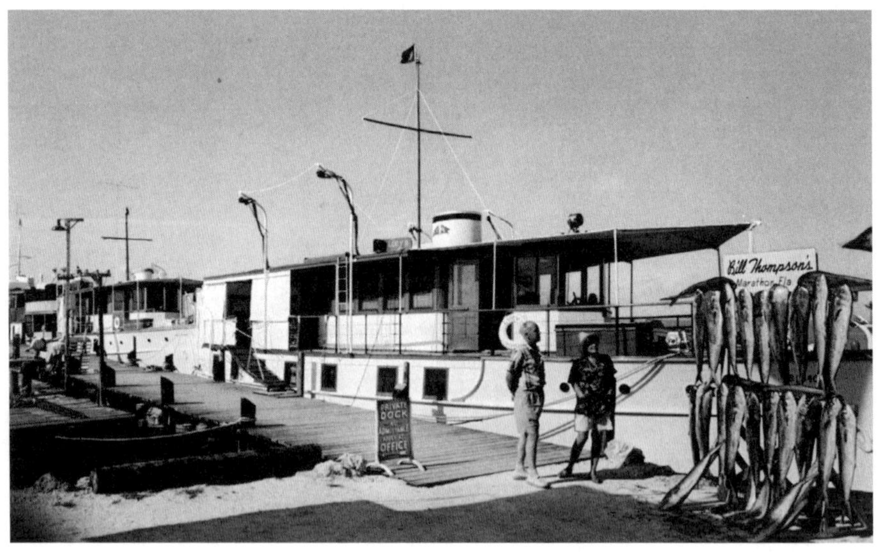

Thompson's Docks, the marina and resort owned by Bill and Ethel Thompson. *Jerry Wilkinson Collection.*

that the metal salvagers had missed. He came to realize that the presence of cannons indicated that a ship had once wrecked on that site. (While a ship's timbers often deteriorated and disappeared over time, items such as cannons and ballast stones remained.) Now, when they weren't working at the marina, the Thompsons spent their free time scrutinizing the ocean floor. For Bill and Ethel, treasure hunting blossomed into a full-fledged passion. Then, in the late 1940s or early 1950s, while he was "trolling a fish line about the reef,"[205] Bill stumbled on the existence of cannons underwater at another site altogether.

About five nautical miles from Big Pine Key in the Lower Keys, Bill and Ethel made some exciting finds on a reef called Looe Key. They recovered multiple items, including pieces of ship's timber, "corroded iron ballast, dozens of cannon balls of many sizes," along with "a copper hoop from a powder keg," "bits from a Chinese porcelain bowl, the remains of a fine crystal unguent jar, a pewter mug, spun-copper plates and utensils and a brass door knocker."[206] Guests at Thompson's Docks could see certain artifacts on display at the property, while other, more fragile items, Bill and Ethel would show only to select visitors.

Soon Bill Thompson recruited two other amateur enthusiasts, Jane and Barney Crile, who were vacationing at the Thompsons' resort. (Barney Crile was a well-known physician at the prestigious Cleveland Clinic.)[207] The Thompsons' fervor rubbed off on the Criles, who returned to the Middle Keys and spent their next vacation exploring the Looe Key site with the marina owners. Bill also convinced Mendel Peterson, from the Department of History at the Smithsonian, to volunteer part of *his* vacation time in helping to properly identify their finds as well.[208] It was Peterson who, back at the Smithsonian, combing records from the British Royal Navy, came across the name of the mysterious ship and the date of the wreck: the *HMS Looe*, lost at sea in 1744.[209]

Located not very far from Thompson's Docks was another wreck, near the Sombrero Lighthouse, that began to yield even more intriguing finds. Here were ivory tusks brought from Africa to the Americas centuries before. Bill Thompson and others came to call this the "Ivory Wreck," due to the elephant tusks, which was an unusual type of cargo to turn up in the Florida Keys. At the western edge of the Delta Shoal, the wreck site would eventually surrender silver bars, buttons, cannonballs and, perhaps most poignant of all, leg irons. Enslaved African men, women and most probably children had been shackled together aboard the vessel, which wrecked in 1853.[210] All of them presumably drowned. In addition to the ivory tusks Bill Thompson recovered from the site, he kept a sizeable anchor from the Ivory Wreck outdoors at the marina.

While Bill Thompson sometimes worked in conjunction with local professional diver Arthur McKee (who dived the Ivory Wreck as well), he and Ethel were generally drawn to other amateurs—not only the Criles but also another couple, the Links. Edwin Link and his wife, Marion Clayton Link, put in at the Thompsons' Marathon marina several times as they sailed their forty-three-foot boat, *Blue Heron*, between Florida and the Bahamas. It was in 1951 that Bill decided to show Ed and Marion what he had in his office: cannons encrusted with coral, "corroded coins," buttons, a pewter cup and the ivory tusks.[211] The Links listened with mounting excitement as Bill and Ethel described their adventures diving wrecks with the Crile family. Now the Links also wanted to join these expeditions.

Both Ed and Marion Link were exceptional people, she an accomplished writer and journalist and he a world-renowned inventor. Before World War II, Ed had invented the famed Link trainer, which the U.S. Army Air Forces came to use to train pilots to fly. He also developed "new types of aviation instruments and equipment, a bubble sextant for use in aircraft, and more efficiently arranged instrument panels and cockpits" that helped the U.S. military during World War II.[212] When Ed and Marion took up sailboat racing, he applied his inventor's mind and knowledge of air navigation to the task of sea navigation. By the time they tied up in Marathon in the spring of 1951, however, Ed Link had grown somewhat bored of racing and was looking for a new pursuit. Coincidentally, before they had taken out *Blue Heron*, he had "stowed a heavy metal diving helmet and a crude hand-operated compressor in the forward hatch."[213]

At the time, most treasure hunters in the Florida Keys had to contend with cumbersome equipment: a diving helmet, an air hose attached to a compressor and weights to keep the diver from bobbing to the ocean's surface. What's more, instead of wearing bathing suits, the divers Marion Link first encountered usually went down fully clothed, with shoes on their feet. The clothing at least offered some protection from rough corals, sea urchins and jellyfish.

Ed Link gladly volunteered to bring the *Blue Heron* to a site on the Delta Shoal, not far from the Ivory Wreck site; at this point, Bill Thompson's group had ballooned to about thirty people. Marion Clayton Link, while plenty adventurous herself, had reservations because, as she later recalled in her book *Sea Diver*, "I was a very poor swimmer." Nevertheless, she "was keenly interested in the romance of an adventure involving sunken ships, the lure of possible treasure finds, and the sudden, mysterious disappearance of ancient Spanish galleons, pirate ships, slavers and square-rigged men-of-war into the sea."[214] Despite worrying about barracuda and sharks, not to mention the possibility of her air hose kinking, she was game for the challenge. For her first dive, Marion did not don an awkward helmet but rather an innovative Desco mask: "a triangle of glass edged with black rubber, equipped with intake and exhaust valves and connected to a hundred feet of hose."[215] She wore jeans and canvas sneakers, in stark contrast to modern-day divers' sleek wetsuits. Despite some panicky moments, she managed to complete a short dive and marveled at the brilliant colors of the corals and fish. That same day, the team aboard *Blue Heron* excitedly recovered a cannon that bore the date 1617.

The hunt for shipwrecks and long-forgotten treasure became all-consuming. As Ed Link mastered the Aqualung (an early tank-diving method), Marion grew into a capable diver and swimmer. They soon set about improving on the strategies that Bill Thompson had been using to discover treasure. First, the couple tried spotting wrecks from the air in their five-seater seaplane, a Grumman Widgeon. (Although the plane flew too quickly to inspect the minute variations of the seafloor, they did once use the seaplane to scare off fishermen who were about to move a marker

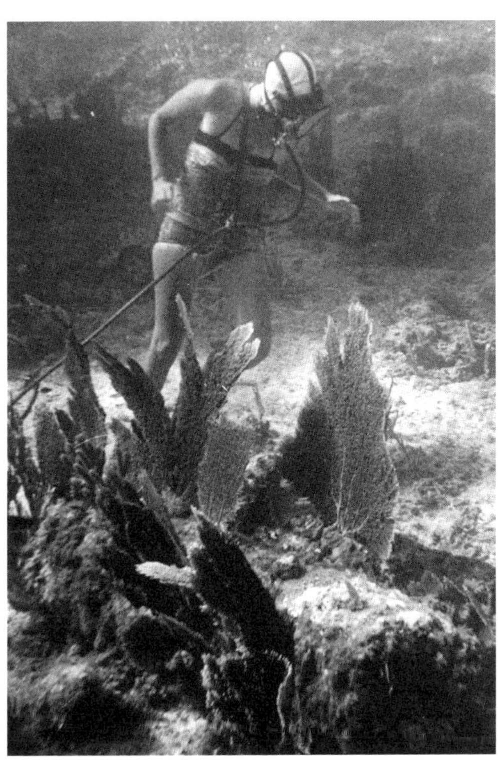

Left: Marion Link searching the sea floor. *Edwin A. and Marion C. Link Collection, Florida Institute of Technology.*

Below: The Links' trawler, *Sea Diver*, at sunset. *Edwin A. and Marion C. Link Collection, Florida Institute of Technology.*

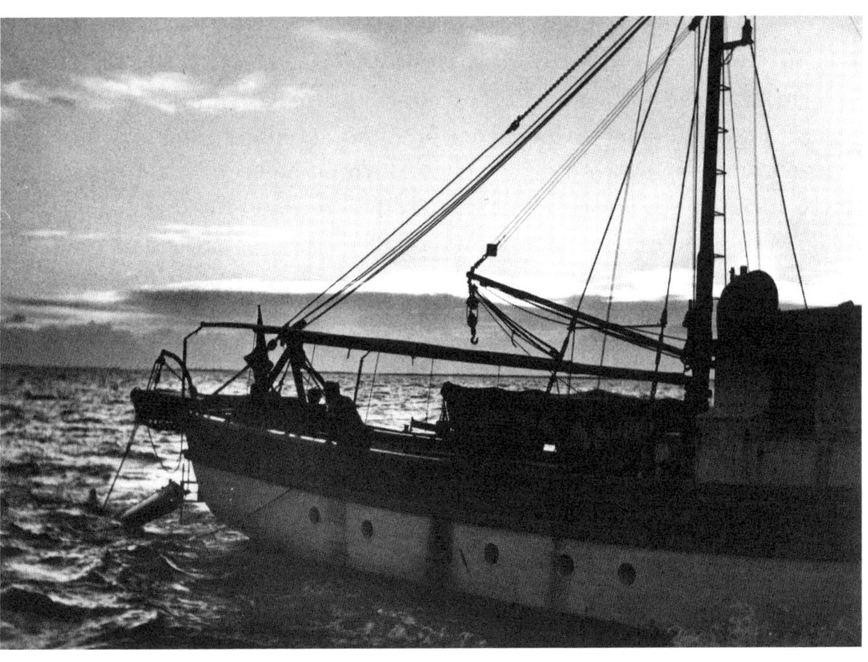

from a wreck site.) The next effort involved another type of technology. Ed decided that they were missing too much trying to spot cannons and ballast with the naked eye. Instead, he brought in a metal detector "which he had rebuilt from a type of land-mine detector developed during World War II." Although the detector could only locate metal over a matter of a few feet, it marked a genuine leap forward.

The Links found that their elegant *Blue Heron* was not suited to retrieving and transporting heavy finds such as cannons. Instead, they borrowed a seventy-five-foot cruiser, *Eryholme*, from a friend and fitted it out with davits so they could also transport a glass-bottom boat that Ed was devising to help them search the ocean floor. Although the *Eryholme* was an improvement, they eventually purchased a sixty-five-foot trawler and former shrimper that they rechristened *Sea Diver*. They fitted the sturdy trawler out for treasure hunting and even installed a crow's nest some thirty-five feet above the deck to give them a better view of the sea bottom when the water was calm.

When the basic metal detector became too limiting, Ed and the Smithsonian's Mendel Peterson persuaded the navy to lend them a magnetometer-gradiometer. That the navy would be willing to send the two men this valuable equipment was a testament to Ed Link's wartime contributions and Mendel Peterson's former service as a naval officer. The naval magnetometer-gradiometer consisted of a "four-foot long cylindrical tube" and an indicator box with dials and switches that required Ed to make constant adjustments.[216] It turned out that the device was so finicky the navy had virtually given up on it. With some effort, inventor Ed Link managed to make it work.

The magnetometer (which later became standard issue for undersea treasure hunters) helped their searches enormously. Yet once the instrument found metal, it still took sifting through the sand and broken shells on the seafloor by hand in order to discover smaller treasure, particularly valuable objects such as gold coins or jewelry. This laborious process cost them too much time, especially when divers needed to wait for windows of good weather. Nevertheless, the Links did make various finds, including a 1751 ship's bell and a Queen Anne–period teapot, which they sent to Mendel Peterson for the Smithsonian's collection.

Edwin Link's intelligent use of technology and redesign or adaptation of equipment could not fail to impress even a professional diver like Arthur "Art" McKee. New Jersey native Art McKee had moved to South Florida, where he first worked as a lifeguard before becoming a professional diver.[217] At first Art recovered underwater ship's cannons only "to collect scrap metal for the war effort."[218] During World War II, he also worked on the water

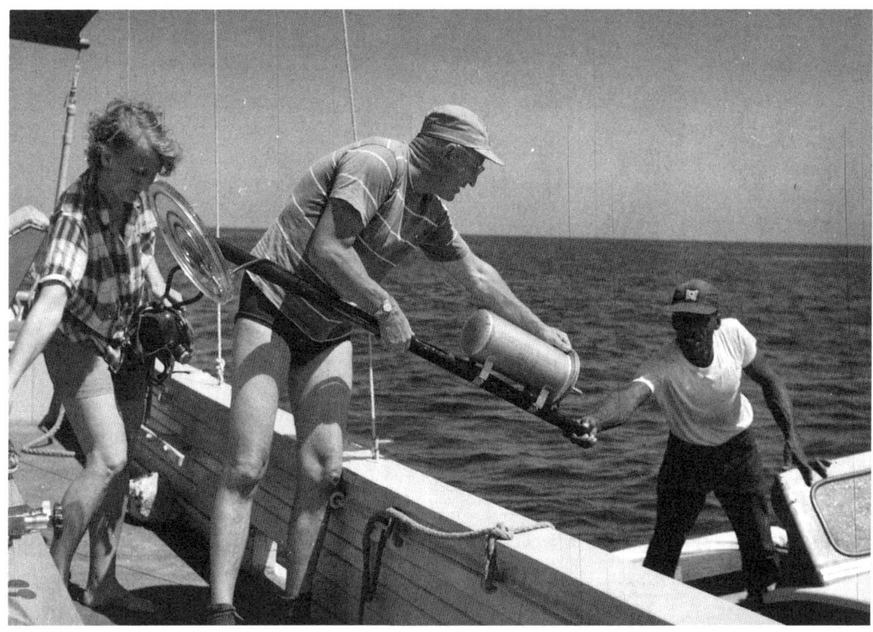

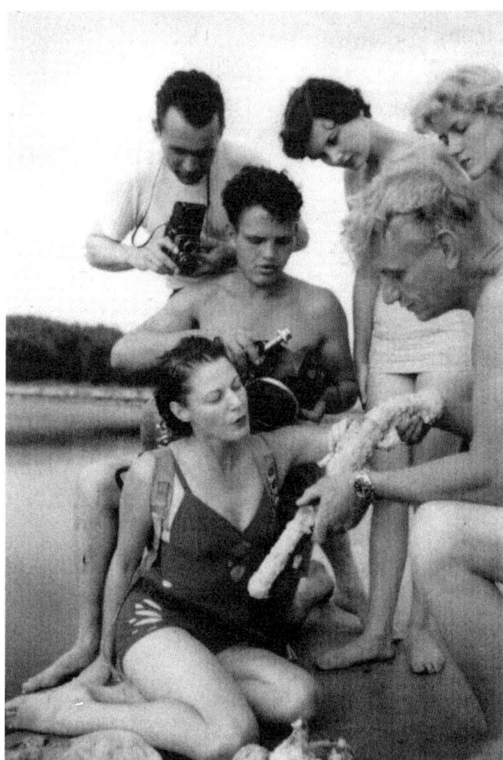

Above: Ed and Marion Link prepare to go aboard the ship *Reef Diver*. *Edwin A. and Marion C. Link Collection, Florida Institute of Technology.*

Left: Treasure hunter Art McKee displays a coral-encrusted pistol to his wife, Gay, and others. *Courtesy of the State Archives of Florida.*

pipeline that would bring fresh water to the Keys. It was a fishing guide, Reggie Roberts, who introduced Art to the 1733 wreck site of *El Capitana* off Tavernier Key, where the diver would go on to make many finds.[219] When Ed and Marion Link met Art, the diver had already recovered a number of artifacts and opened his Museum of Sunken Treasure, at that time a little building on Plantation Key. His initial display included two silver bars.

While the Thompsons and the Links had been searching for shipwrecks for the thrill of discovery, diver Art McKee was turning the hunt for undersea treasure into a career. In a highly strategic move, he acquired an exclusive permit from the State of Florida to salvage "an area reaching from Key Largo well south of Hen and Chickens [reef] and extending seaward toward the reefs" in the early 1950s.[220] The others had not seen this coming. Now, the sites that the Thompsons, the Links, the Criles and Mendel Peterson had been diving were "Art's wrecks"—a dramatic change. Art invited both the Links and the Smithsonian's Mendel Peterson to join him on expeditions in the summers of 1953 and 1954, when he took out his ship, *Treasure Princess*. In return for his generosity, the Links supplied Art "with an additional jetting hose and the metal detector."[221] At the time, both the Links and Art McKee were using hoses to dislodge sand from the seafloor, but the hoses' action seemed to force artifacts further beneath the sand. Again, Ed Link's technological brilliance came to the rescue: he created an "air lift" to "suck up the sand through a big pipe and redeposit it at a safe distance," while installing a screen over the pipe so that while the sand filtered through, objects remained behind.[222] Using these hoses with powerful suction, they found a melted gold doubloon from the 1730s. Certainly, the air lift transformed the process of scouring sites along the Florida Reef.

But the Links had to face the fact that they no longer had autonomy to explore these Florida Keys wreck sites, except with the express permission—and under the supervision—of Art McKee. Disappointed by this restriction, they decided that it was time to take *Sea Diver* elsewhere to hunt for history that lay hidden beneath the waves. On a new expedition in the Bahamas, Ed and Marion were joined by the Criles and continued to collaborate with Mendel Peterson and send him artifacts for the Smithsonian.

Over the next decades, Peterson conducted numerous expeditions (including a few with the Links) in the West Indies and around the world; he helped design a grid system to survey marine sites that is still used today. Over time, he would become a respected pioneer in the field of underwater archaeology while authoring books on the subject and serving as the Smithsonian's curator of the Division of Historic Archaeology.

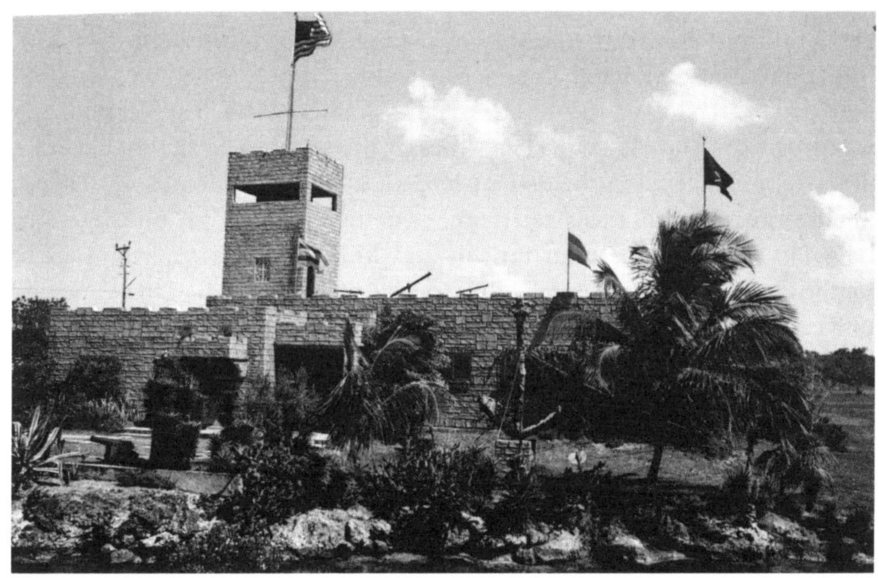

Art McKee designed his new museum to look like a castle. *Jerry Wilkinson Collection.*

As for Ed Link, the celebrated inventor later developed submersible decompression chambers, submersibles used for lockout diving and an unmanned Cable Observation and Rescue Device (CORD). His far-reaching legacy would encompass not only aviation but also submersibles and underwater archaeology. One can only speculate what more the Links might have contributed to Florida Reef exploration had they remained in the region.

Meanwhile, Art McKee proved himself a savvy businessman, selling twenty thousand shares in the treasure museum company.[223] It turned out to be a case of perfect timing, as the public's fascination with treasure hunting grew, and his name became more and more well known. Art would eventually discover so many silver bars that people took to calling him Art "Silver Bar" McKee. Success allowed him to commission a much larger museum, built like a replica of a storybook castle, to attract tourists traveling on the Overseas Highway. (Today, it houses an Islamorada school, around mile marker 86.)

For a time one of the Keys' most famous figures, McKee died in 1980 at the age of sixty-nine. After his death, it seemed that people might forget about Art McKee, his star eclipsed by the staggering finds of Mel Fisher. Yet over the past years, Florida Keys historians such as Jerry Wilkinson and Brad Bertelli and the History of Diving Museum in Islamorada have brought new attention to his story. Meanwhile, Mendel Peterson's research and letters survive in the Smithsonian's archives, and his exceptionally well-researched work, "The Last Voyage of the H.M.S. 'Looe,'" can be accessed online. Bill and Ethel Thompson's marina, Thompson's Docks, on the other hand, exists no more, and their pioneering investigations have largely been forgotten. Edwin and Marion Link's contributions to underwater exploration survive in special collections at more than one university library, yet few remember that this brilliant couple made such a mark on treasure hunting in the Florida Keys.

Chapter 9

Exotics in the Tropics

From its founding in the nineteenth century, Key West has seen no shortage of exotic individuals, but few could outdo burlesque dancer Sally Rand. This petite, blond-haired dynamo regularly performed for attentive crowds at the rollicking Havana Madrid Club.[224] There she would bewitch audiences with her fan dance, maneuvering two pink, seven-foot-tall ostrich fans around her nude figure. Her notorious bubble dance, which featured a translucent, five-foot bubble that Sally designed herself, also won her a raft of devotees.[225] Although frequently labeled an "exotic dancer" by the press, the performer wasn't especially fond of the term. "The dictionary defines 'exotic' as that which is strange and foreign," Sally Rand once retorted. "I am not strange; I like boys. I am not foreign; I was born and raised in Hickory County, Missouri." With her all-American looks, quick wit and hypnotic routines, she quickly became the toast of Key West.

Unlike some artists who only blitzed through town, Sally Rand made the island a part-time home from the 1940s through the early 1950s. She visited the wounded and ill at the Key West Naval Hospital and taught little children dance moves at Casa Marina. After World War II, she bought a two-story Conch house at 916 Eisenhower Drive, where she raised her adopted son, Sean Orion.[226]

Sally befriended one of the most socially prominent Conchs in town, Jessie Porter Newton, and because a regular at her parties.[227] In turn, "Miss Jessie" attended Sally's shows, which attracted not only the usual bar-hopping suspects but also a well-heeled, upscale crowd. Spectators who

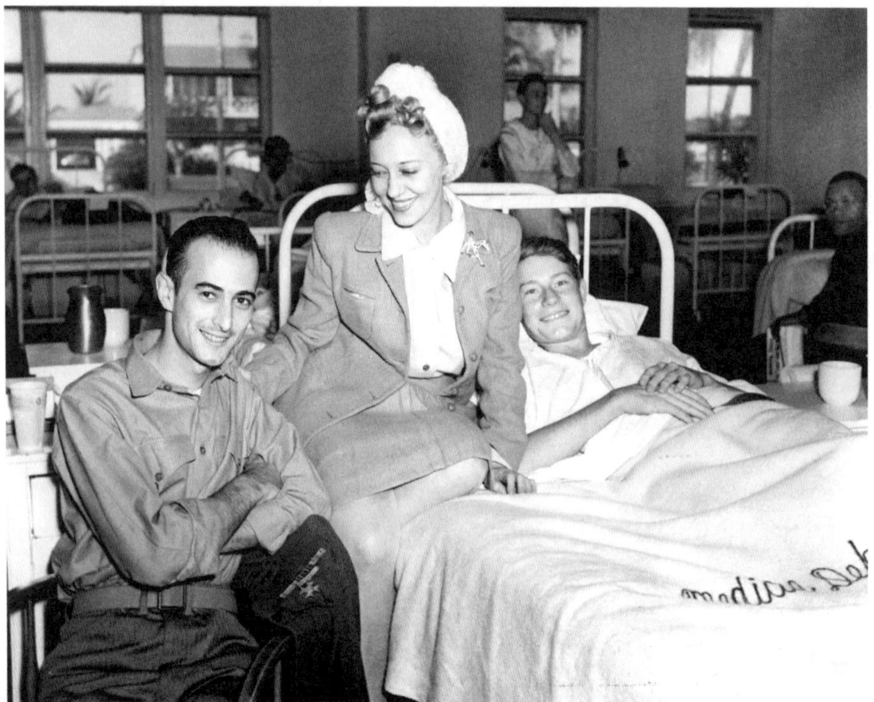

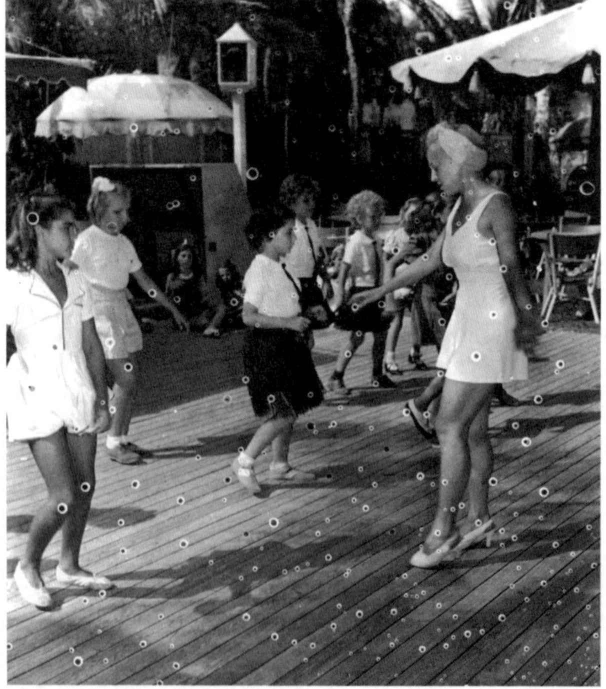

Above: Sally Rand visits the Naval Hospital in Key West. *Courtesy of the Monroe County Public Library, Key West.*

Left: Sally Rand teaches children dance steps at Casa Marina. *Courtesy of the Monroe County Public Library, Key West.*

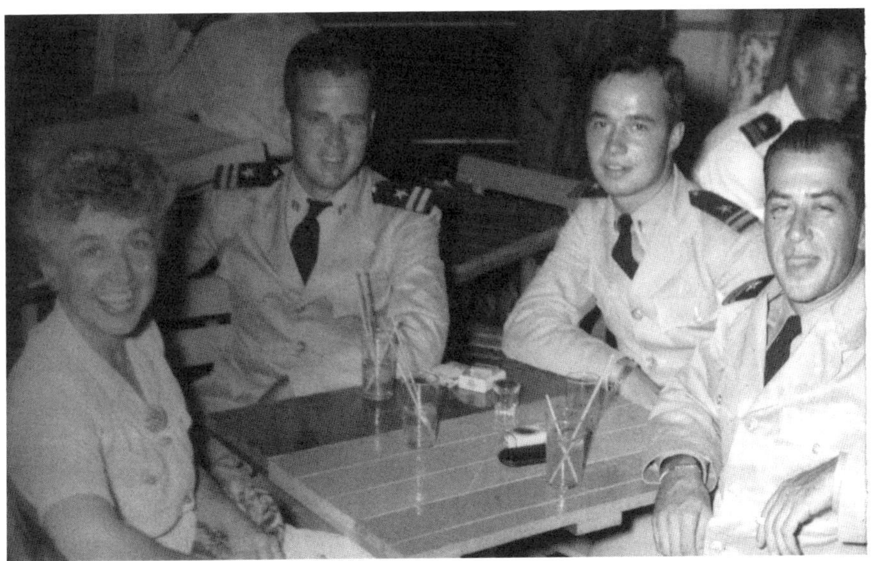

Jessie Porter and friends at a nightclub where Sally Rand performed. *Courtesy of the Monroe County Public Library, Key West.*

came expecting a lewd strip tease or bump-and-grind were disappointed: Sally sometimes performed her fan dance to the sublime strains of Debussy's "Claire de Lune."[228] Her originality endeared her to Key Westers, who welcomed her back with enthusiasm each winter season.

As a young woman, Sally Rand enrolled in college but had to drop out for lack of money. Initially, she hoped to become a ballet dancer or a serious actress. Early in her career, she took to acting onstage—including in one production opposite Humphrey Bogart—and starred in silent Hollywood films.[229] Director Cecil B. DeMille was the one who christened five-foot-one Missouri native Helen Beck the more memorable "Sally Rand." (Allegedly, a Rand-McNally atlas inspired the last name.[230]) The Great Depression put a damper on her more conventional ambitions, and her lisp prevented her from transitioning from silent films to talkies. But she needed to earn a living. After venturing into burlesque, her career soared. Sally ultimately became a pop culture icon and later noted, "I haven't been out of work since the day I took my pants off." She would marry three times and continued dancing well into her sixties.

Like audiences all over America, Key Westers wondered: Did Sally, in fact, reveal all, or was it only an illusion? Her famous retort to busybodies who pressed the point was, "The Rand is quicker than the eye." Although viewers may have believed they saw more, generally she revealed just some leg or a glimpse of her bottom.[231] A sheer body stocking or pale powder covered her during performances.[232] A Key West fixture for more than a decade, she eventually moved away and retired to California. Few traces of her exist on the island, although her home on Eisenhower Drive, now renovated, still stands. Watch an online video of Sally at the 1934 World's Fair to get a glimpse of the all-American exotic who once danced enchanted circles around Key West's locals.

In the early 1940s, not just anyone embarked on a new life in the Middle Keys. Of course, these largely undeveloped islands offered visitors the promise of year-round sunshine, Caribbean blue–tinged waters, world-class fishing and a landscape of tropical flowers and palm trees. Beginning in the late 1930s, an overseas highway and bridges connected the islands to one another and to the mainland. But conditions could be basic. Residents collected fresh water in rain barrels and relied on generators for electricity or used kerosene lanterns at night. No one had air conditioning, and the Middle Keys had long been known as a magnet for particularly vicious swarms of mosquitoes.

Nevertheless, the islands' beauty and relative seclusion proved irresistible to a certain type of person, and soon businesses sprouted alongside of the road. There were practical endeavors, like a sundry store and fish packing facility, but also rowdy fish camps, restaurants with key lime pie and, of course, the inevitable bars. In Marathon, the Overseas Lounge appeared in the 1930s, and in the next decade, Gil and Maud Spence's Flamingo Bar and Restaurant opened.

An unprepossessing place on the outside, the Flamingo featured a long bar with a giant tropical mural, and pictures, drawings and doodles all crowded together on the walls. People came for the company and especially for the cocktails. (A sign over the doors read, "Through these portals many famous people have passed out.") Soon, people came for another attraction: the Snake Lady. Her real name was Alma Cagle Bishop, and she did not follow the conventional 1940s rule book. When she arrived in Marathon, rumors suggested that Alma had been married once or possibly twice. But in Marathon, she appeared to be decisively single, without kids or any of the ordinary trappings of domestic life.

In the fairly quiet Upper and Middle Keys, word spread about a woman who entertained people in the Flamingo with dangerous-looking reptiles.

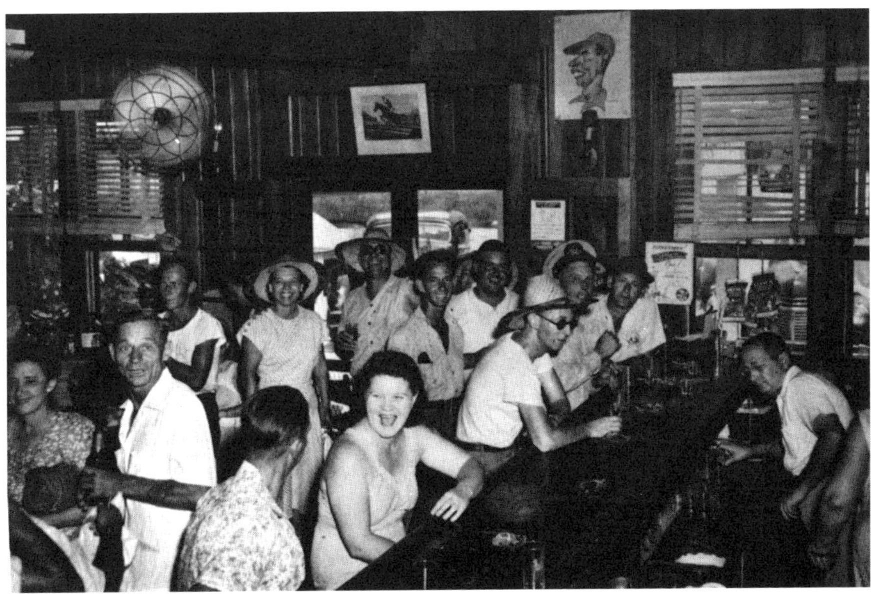

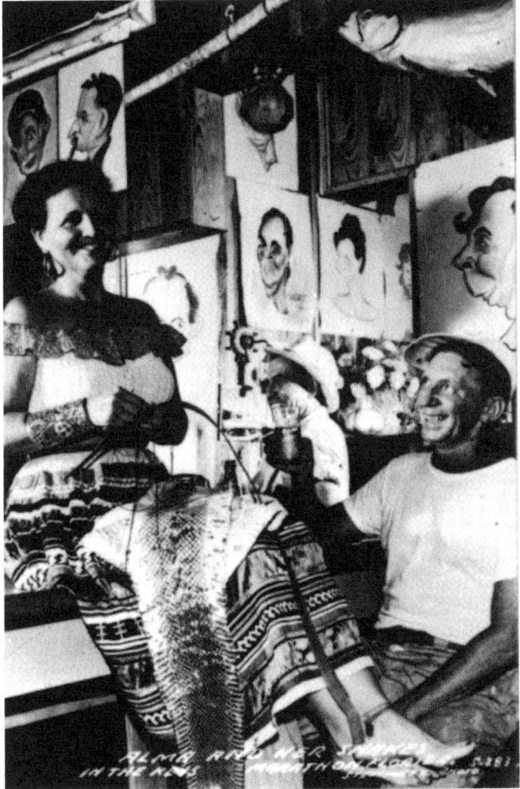

Above: The Flamingo Bar was one of Marathon's most happening spots. *Courtesy of the Monroe County Public Library, Key West.*

Left: Alma Cagle Bishop at the Flamingo Bar with a snakeskin on her lap. *Courtesy of the Monroe County Public Library, Key West.*

With her curly brown hair and charming smile, Alma was her own best PR agent. Tourists and locals flocked to the bar, drank something cold, icy and alcoholic and watched goggle-eyed as this gregarious bohemian handled snakes as though they were beloved pets. She expressed no fear. At home, she kept her slithering "pretties" in her bathtub. While traveling away from Marathon, she simply stuck some snakes in a pillowcase. Before long, Alma the Snake Lady had become one of the Florida Keys' most popular roadside attractions.

In Alma's case, the snakes weren't run-of-the-mill pets, however, because she would eventually kill them off. The main moneymaking arm of her business was selling wallets, belts and other wares crafted from snakeskin. She raised the reptiles, showed them off inside the Flamingo and then finally sliced them up, cured the skin and sewed them into something tourists would gladly buy.

In her brightly colored Seminole Indian skirt, Alma was the center of attention as much as her snakes. People couldn't fail to notice that sometimes she wore exotic black fingernail polish—decades before black polish had a fashion moment. She took lovers freely, picking them and dropping them as the inclination moved her. She drank and she swore. Perhaps this wasn't how respectable women in the 1940s and '50s were supposed to behave, but Alma quite frankly did not give a damn.

Besides the snakes, she owned an adorable miniature marmoset monkey named Freddie. She even called her stand inside the Flamingo "Freddie's Gift Shop." Monkeys were not exactly thick on the ground in the Florida Keys, and Freddie became a minor Marathon celebrity too. Alma also owned a horse, which grazed across the street from the Flamingo Bar while she worked. She trotted it up and down the Keys at a time when horses on the road had become an oddity. One day, she rode the horse right into a Key West bar. No doubt the act won her another string of admirers. Men may have desired her, but more than a few women must have envied her freedom and her charisma.

Alma not only supported herself but also achieved an amount of local fame while living exactly the way she wanted. Her life came to a tragic end in 1975 when she was struck on the road by a car. She was buried on Big Pine Key. Ernest Hemingway once wrote, "Nobody ever lives their life all the way up except bullfighters." Alma Cagle Bishop may have disagreed.

IN THE PROHIBITION ERA, AND later in the late 1960s, '70s and '80s, Key West developed a reputation as a place where people might go more than a little wild. (In fact, some went right off the rails.) Stories accumulated of outrageous partying, and these true tales often involved quantities of alcohol or illegal narcotics. Some of those who misbehaved were artists, while others merely aspired to live "artistically." But the island did not always have the same disorienting effect on every new arrival.

By 1957, dark-haired Bettie Page had been the leading American pinup for most of the decade. Born in Tennessee during the Depression, Bettie, like Sally Rand, first aspired to act in mainstream Hollywood films. After an unsuccessful screen test at Paramount Pictures, she moved to New York, where she found a more mundane job. But her dramatic looks and sensational body attracted the attention of amateur photographers. First, she posed for amateurs at photo clubs and then professionals—initially in bikinis and later in the nude. "I don't believe God disapproves of nudity," Bettie would remark later in life. "He put Adam and Eve in the Garden of Eden, naked as jaybirds."[233] She appeared on the covers of hundreds of magazines and in several 8mm burlesque films; Hugh Heffner made her one of *Playboy* magazine's first centerfolds. Eventually, her career expanded into fetish and bondage.

Bettie Page might have been an island-wide sensation had her arrival been announced in the *Key West Citizen* or on the radio. But that's not how it happened. By 1957, she was thirty-four years old; she had fled New York and abandoned her successful pinup career, her own version of a mid-life crisis after intense years full of work and notoriety. The government was cracking down on suggestive images, including those of Bettie Page. Low on money and at loose ends in Fort Lauderdale, she telephoned a Conch named Armond Carlyle Walterson.[234] She and Armond had enjoyed a brief romance years earlier in Miami, and now Bettie needed a refuge. With an invitation from Armond to live in Key West at his house on Elizabeth Street, she boarded a bus and took the road trip down the Overseas Highway.

Soon the notorious Bettie Page had been embraced by Armond's whole family, including his eleven sisters and brothers. They held big picnics on Boca Chica, where they "had sack races and jump rope competitions on the beach."[235] Playing purely for fun on the sand was a world away from posing with whips for fetish shots in New York City, but Bettie had always had two sides: the wholesome, all-American girl with bangs and a wide, cheerful grin and the vixen who might indulge in a round of onscreen spanking. Armond's large family may have reminded her of her own childhood (although her

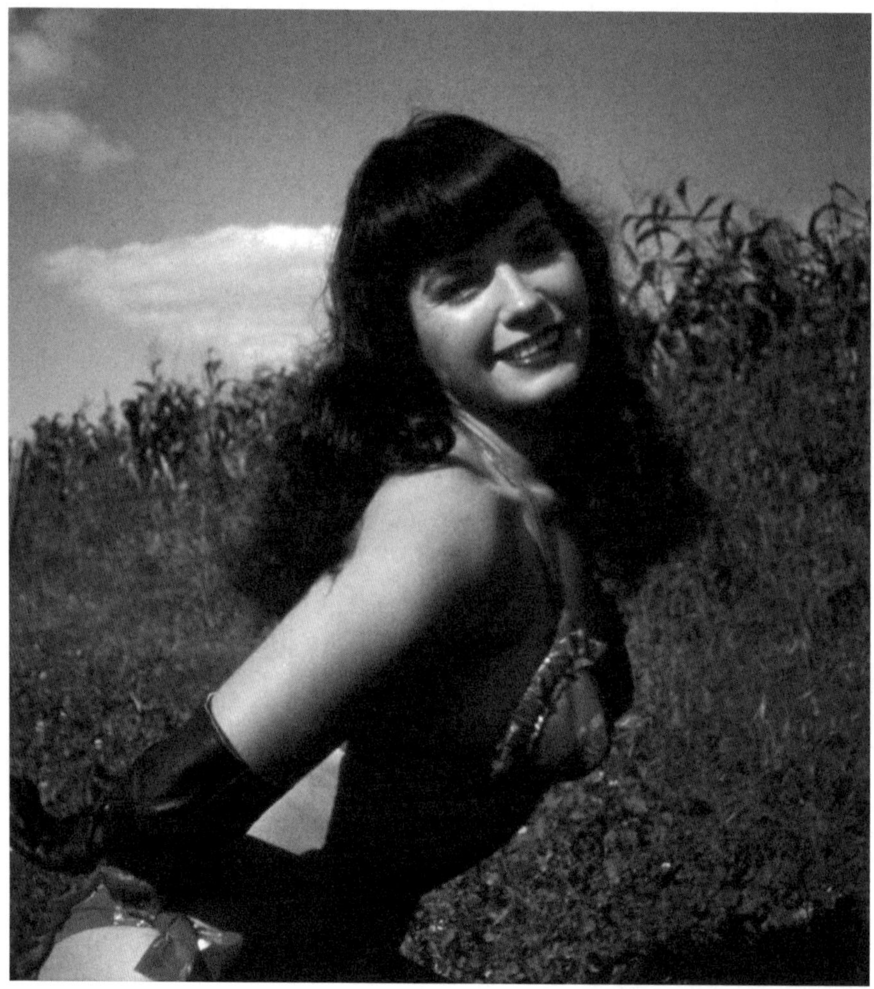

Pinup celebrity Bettie Page escaped to Key West. *Courtesy of Wikimedia, Creative Commons Attribution-Share Alike 3.0 Unported.*

own southern family had financial troubles and Bettie was even placed for a time in an orphanage). Unfortunately, she suffered a serious injury playing volleyball; a period of being confined to a wheelchair for four months only cemented the end of her career in front of the camera.[236] Without her usual way of supporting herself, Bettie began to look for work in Key West. Since she had taught school before, she applied in June 1958 to teach elementary school in the Monroe County school system.[237] She herself had been a top student, serving on student council in high school and also editing the school newspaper. Bettie also held a bachelor's degree from Peabody College.[238] The pinup star was hired. The staff in charge of recruitment apparently did not recognize one of the most photographed faces in America.

On August 15, Bettie Page arrived in a classroom full of fifth graders at Harris Elementary. Maintaining order quickly became a problem. One older student, the son of a naval officer, had failed fifth grade so many times than at this point, he was a teenager. He and other rambunctious students made teaching hell for her. "I lasted just one term," Bettie later recalled. "I had a very rowdy bunch of students in my class....I was very disappointed in my teaching experience and didn't care to pursue it any further."[239] Instead, Bettie managed to get a job working at the Key West Naval Base; she typed and filed papers for the director of public works, J.S. Meggs. This latest job lasted nine months.

At the time, it would have surprised her avid fans to learn that Bettie Page quietly married her boyfriend, Armond, in Key West's First Methodist Church. Just as she had once made her burlesque costumes, Bettie sewed her own wedding dress out of pale silk.[240] Although like any newlyweds they dreamed of future happiness, sadly, the marriage didn't last. In fact, on New Year's Eve 1958, Bettie and Armond started arguing. He wanted to celebrate at a pal's house, while Betty wished to dance the night away at a club.[241] Further complicating the situation was the fact that his wife preferred that he not drink—even on New Year's Eve. Eventually, Armond went his own way, while Bettie threw on some old clothes and headed down to the water. "I was going to lie down on the wall and listen to the ocean and look at the stars and think of whether or not that I was going to leave Armon [*sic*]," she would remember.[242] Some would later claim that she felt suicidal that night, but Bettie refuted that idea. She simply wanted to reassess her life. But as she continued down White Street, "It was like somebody took me by the hand and guided me across the street and I saw a little church over there with a door open and heard music, singing. It had a white, neon-lit cross over the top of it. It was a little Latin American Baptist temple."

A preacher named Morris Wright led the service, although he usually preached on Stock Island.[243] In the back of the simple church, Bettie stood and listened to the reverend speak of salvation. At one point, she felt tears form in her eyes. The urgent words of his sermon moved her, as had the hymns. She would recall that "I stood back there and cried about all my sins, and I thought God disapproved of me doing nudes, you know. I didn't think anything about the fetish and the bondage...because I had to do that, but I thought maybe he looked down on me for posing in the nude."[244] Two nights later, Bettie Page returned to the little church and accepted Jesus Christ as her savior.

With her new faith and the recognition that the marriage with Armond would never work, Bettie Page made her getaway from Key West. She told her husband she was going to spend time with her mother in Tennessee. Hoping for a reunion, Armond drove up to Tennessee after her, only to learn from her mother that Bettie had actually moved to California. She and Armond divorced. Then Bettie threw herself into religion, studying at Bible schools and trying to become a missionary to Africa. (Unfortunately, the missionaries did not approve of divorced women.) She also struggled for a time with mental illness. Later in life, when her stature as a cult figure grew, she embraced the work she had done as a pinup and in film. That was when she decided that God did not disapprove of nudity after all. Bettie Page passed away in 2008, but her legend lives on. Books and graphic novels about her still appear, along with films and fashion tributes. In addition to that fame, Bettie also holds the distinction of being a rather unusual onetime Key West resident: she arrived with a notorious past and left squeaky clean.

Chapter 10

Saving History

Imagine walking along Key West's Fleming Street, and instead of elegant two-story Conch houses, the only buildings you pass are concrete-block motels. Picture strolling on Simonton, where the few surviving wood-frame buildings appear bare of paint, shutters swinging off their hinges, gingerbread trim damaged or missing. Then envisage going over to Mallory Square, and instead of a wide plaza where people gather to watch the sun set, the only view is of oil silos and machinery. These scenarios are not as implausible as they sound. Key West's historic charm and character were once in danger of being lost forever.

Key West's economy has always experienced cycles of boom and bust, and this financial seesawing inevitably affected the built environment. During the Great Depression, many of the island's historic homes became derelict: salt air, termites, a lack of funds and time itself took a toll on the buildings, from Front Street to United Street. In the 1930s, the Works Progress Administration descended on a bankrupt Key West and helped restore a limited number of the island's historic properties. Then, with the influx of navy personnel and civilians during World War II, money flowed into the island. Key Westers could once again afford to do the ongoing maintenance required to keep up their historic houses. After the war, however, with the postwar economic boom, Americans wanted "the new," the modern, the sleek and coolly futuristic. Old-time architecture such as that found in Key West was simply not in fashion.

By the late 1950s and into the 1960s, parts of Old Town Key West began to look increasingly decrepit. Houses turned gray, and the unpainted wood took a beating from the elements. Even the streets themselves started to show signs of neglect. Duval Street gradually went from being the island's bustling "Main Street" to a forlorn avenue that some locals were embarrassed by. With the navy's numbers dwindling and businesses leaving the Old Town district, the time appeared right (at least to certain people) to sweep many of those unkempt historical relics right off the island. Not everyone felt like that, of course, but in sleepy, down-at-heels Key West, many Conchs did not harbor any particular pride in the Classic Revival Conch houses, Queen Anne–style mansions or Cuban cigar workers' cottages.

Fortunately, there were still residents who could look at a city block of tired, ramshackle homes and see their potential splendor. Fifth-generation Conch Jessie Porter descended from prominent Key Westers, including millionaire William Curry and Dr. Joseph Y. Porter, the doctor who helped stamp out yellow fever in Key West. At first, she started preservation on a small, manageable scale: in the 1930s, she and her husband, Wallace Kirke, purchased the 1834 Captain Carey House at 410 Caroline Street.[245] The house itself was a mess, but with the help of carpenter Joe Hannibal, Jessie Porter Kirke undertook a total restoration. In the end, 410 Caroline Street was transformed into one of the island's handsomest homes, decorated with period furniture and artwork.

Gregarious, with sparkling eyes, "Miss Jessie" (as she was known) was a natural-born ringleader and organizer. The house on Caroline Street soon became a cultural hub, filled with fascinating people. Her friend, the poet Robert Frost, spent sixteen winters writing in a cottage on the property.[246] Over the course of an evening at Miss Jessie's, one might see playwright Tennessee Williams, philosopher John Dewey and exotic dancer Sally Rand among a crowd hobnobbing over cocktails. In addition to amassing remarkable friends and giving them a social haven, Miss Jessie also accumulated historic buildings.

After her first husband died, Jessie Porter Kirke married a wealthy Kentucky oilman, E.L. Newton. Some of that oil money would eventually be siphoned off to aid historic Key West. Meanwhile, as the *Miami Herald* would chronicle, in 1950s Key West, "housewrecking was becoming almost as popular as salvaging ship wrecks had been a century before."[247] When Miss Jessie heard of yet another structure to be torn down, she would attempt to save it in the quickest, most straightforward way possible: by

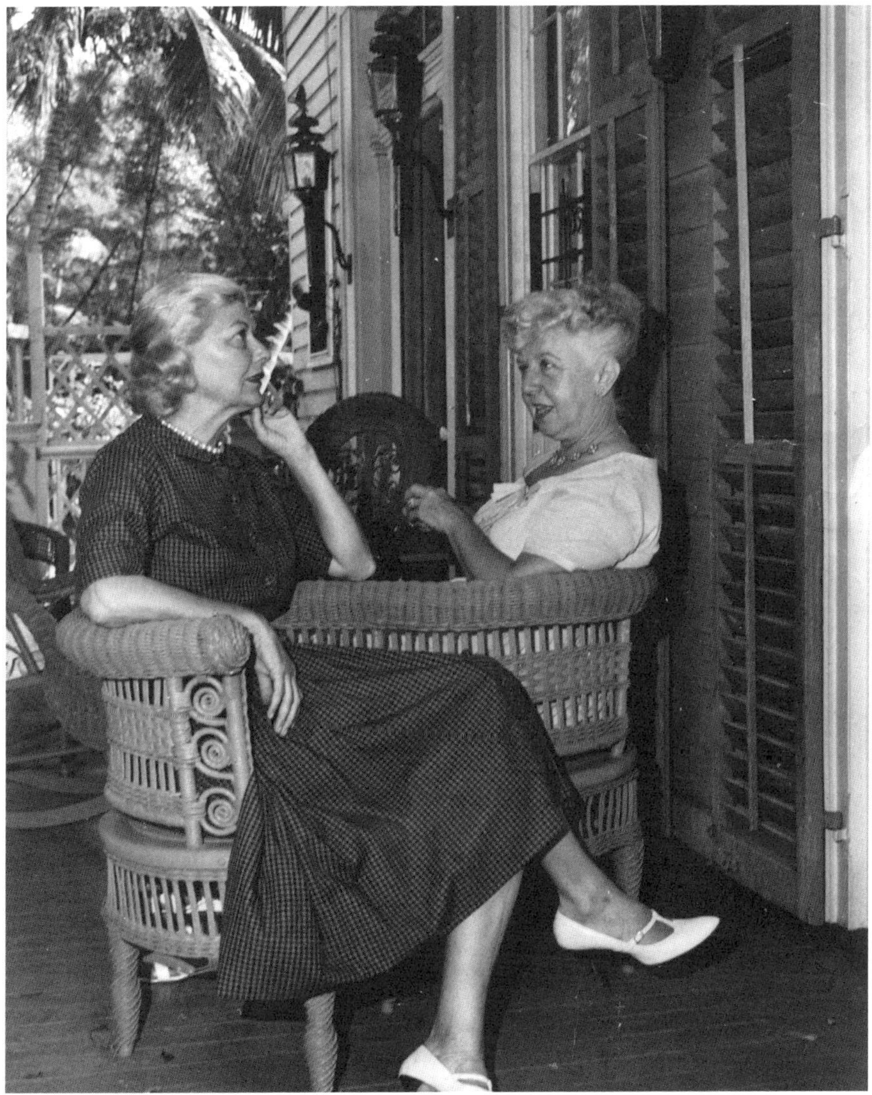

Jessie Porter Kirke Newton (*at right*) felt passionate about preserving Key West's architectural heritage. *Courtesy of the Monroe County Public Library, Key West.*

purchasing the building and having it transported to her land on Caroline Street. "And Newt [her husband] puts up with all this," she mischievously told a reporter.[248] Included in this motley collection were a pigeon house once owned by the Pan American airline, a cigar maker's cottage, a house built by wrecker Braddish Johnson and the Molly Pitcher House, which belonged to the Pitcher family.[249] Jessie had the buildings arranged in landscaped gardens and turned into apartments that she could rent out.

Yet these efforts could not save all the historic treasures from bulldozers and the wrecking ball. One of Key West's first hotels, the Jefferson, stood on the northern section of Duval Street. Erected in 1886, the building had long been an island landmark. It suffered in a fire, however, and in 1958, the grand old structure was unceremoniously torn down. In its place, Southeast Bank installed a drive-up banking window.[250] More and more history fell victim to modernity. Late in the 1950s, a fire damaged the Caroline Lowe House at 303 Duval Street. This home stood just opposite the Dr. Joseph Y. Porter House, which had belonged to Jessie's grandfather, and moreover was just a half block from her own home on Caroline Street.

Local legend had it that one day during the Civil War, as Union troops marched along Duval Street, Confederate sympathizer Caroline Lowe unfurled the Confederate flag from her second-story balcony. Soldiers later searched her home but could not locate the Stars and Bars. She had allegedly secreted the outlawed flag in a hidden compartment within a bannister or, more intriguingly, underneath her hoop skirts. (Caroline Lowe was mother to Alfred Lowe, who joined the Key West Avengers.) Although the legend of the flag waving is most likely a fiction, the Caroline Lowe House was

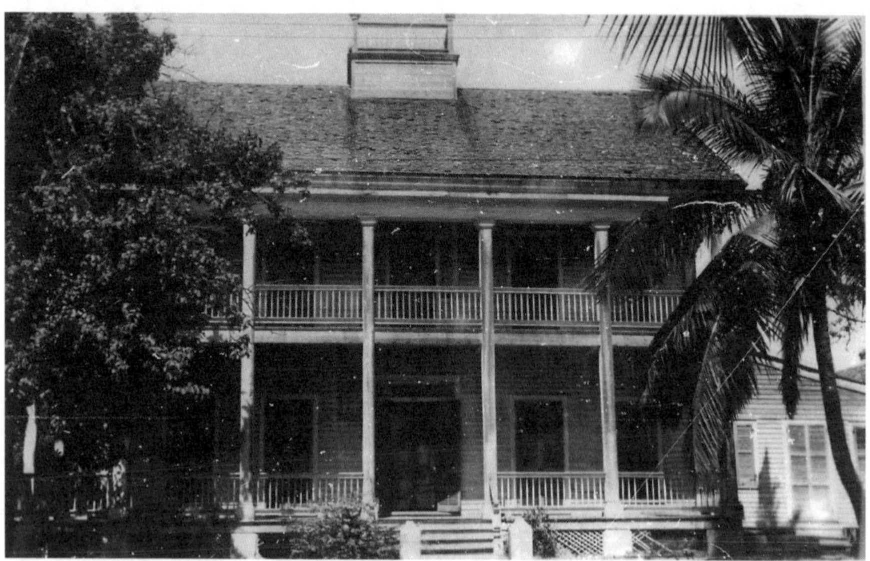

The Caroline Lowe House stood at 303 Duval Street. *Courtesy of the Monroe County Public Library, Key West.*

nevertheless an impressive representation of Key West's unique architecture. Today, such an imposing, nineteenth-century building would be restored; indeed, the fire damage was not severe, and restoration would have been possible.[251] Yet the developer who owned the house planned to rip it down: he had been offered $20,000 for the land itself.[252] The idea of destroying the Caroline Lowe House distressed Jessie Porter Newton terribly. Seeking to save it, she got in touch with the National Trust, and when those efforts did not succeed, she pleaded with the owner to change his mind.

One morning at 6:00 a.m., when it was still dark outside, she awoke to the sounds of demolition. Jessie bolted upright and told her husband, Newt, that she was running out: "I'll go sit and they'll have to bulldoze me, too."[253] Instead, he forbade her to go, most likely to keep her out of danger. Even many years later, the needless destruction of the Caroline Lowe House still infuriated her:

> *You couldn't have built another house like that for $150,000 considering the wood pegs and wood cut by hand. The pillars were solid wood two-and-a-half stories high. There was a crooked coconut palm in the garden and you could see the moon through it. It was so beautiful. When the bulldozers were through, it was just flat dirt.*[254]

If the demise of the Caroline Lowe House disturbed those Key Westers who did love and appreciate their architectural heritage, the impending threat to another home positively horrified them. On the corner of Greene and Whitehead Streets stood the three-story Geiger House, built in 1846 by Captain John Geiger, Key West's first harbor pilot and one of its most prosperous wreckers. Although in need of a great deal of work, the Geiger House had long been one of Key West's loveliest homes. The grounds also had significance: it is believed that John James Audubon used plants from the property as models in certain paintings that became part of his magnum opus, *Birds of America*; Audubon even inserted the property's "Geiger tree" in one piece. Yet the house was slated to be demolished, and in its stead would be a mundane gasoline station.

One reality had become clear: not even E.L. Newton's Kentucky oil money could rescue sufficient numbers of historic homes in Key West. The effort to save buildings one by one by moving them onto Miss Jessie's property was a losing strategy. The Geiger House's looming demolition galvanized her into action.[255] In 1958, Jessie Porter Newton invited a group of like-minded individuals into her back garden for a meeting.[256] On the

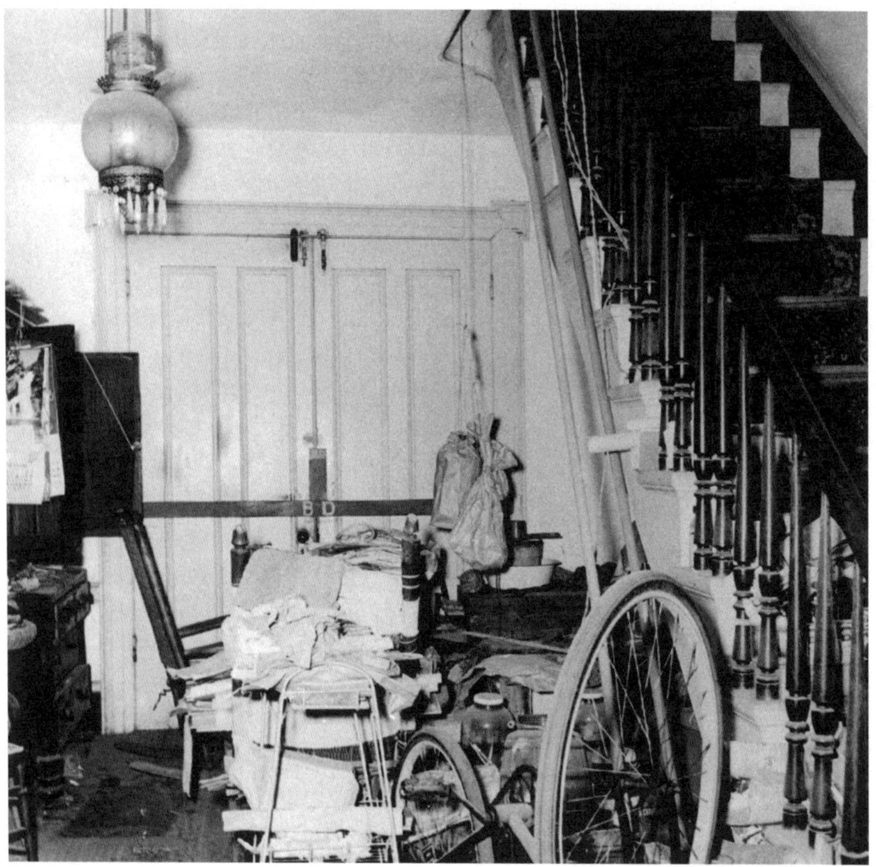

Inside the Geiger House (later Audubon House) before its restoration. *Courtesy of the Monroe County Public Library, Key West.*

agenda was one item: how best to save historic Key West. While one woman might not be able to make significant progress, she knew that a collection of determined, well-connected citizens could succeed. Her invited guests responded with enthusiasm, and they formed a new organization, the Old Island Restoration Foundation.

The first, most urgent task they set themselves was to save the Geiger House. The board members decided that the only person with the potential—and deep enough pockets—to acquire the home and fund the restoration was Mitchell Wolfson. The Key West native certainly had amassed a fortune: he owned a South Florida Coca-Cola distributing company as well as movie theaters; he had also built the Miami Seaquarium.[257] But Wolfson's interests extended to cultural matters, too, and he had founded a museum, the

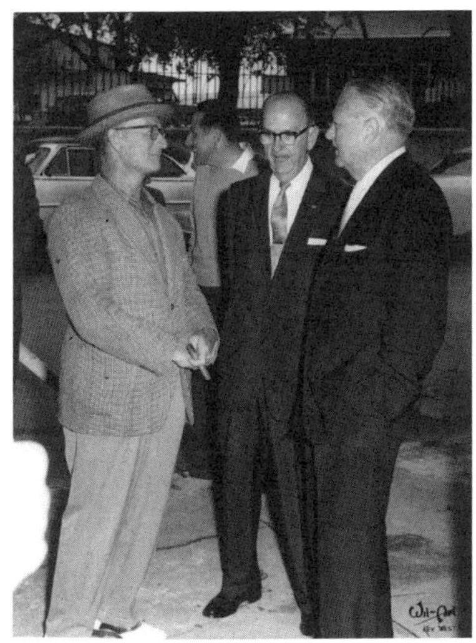

Mitchell Wolfson *(far right)* and his wife, Frances, made the Audubon House restoration possible. *Courtesy of the Monroe County Public Library, Key West.*

Collection of Decorative and Propaganda Arts on Miami Beach, in a restored 1920s building (today the Wolfsonian Museum). According to historian Tom Hambright, one of the women on the Old Island Restoration Foundation's board was married to a close boyhood friend of Mitchell Wolfson's. The board thus convinced the husband to travel to the entrepreneur's office and use all his powers of persuasion. Tom Hambright recalled that the gentleman sat down with Mitchell, who eventually asked him, "What do you want?" to which he replied, "I can't leave until you agree to buy and restore the [Geiger] house."[258] It was a challenge that the businessman could not resist.

With his wife, Frances, Mitchell "Micky" Wolfson contributed about $250,000 (more than $2 million in today's dollars) for a complete restoration of the property. Master craftsman Milton Evans, along with his sons, John and Harry, undertook the massive project. Wolfson could not have hired a more experienced local builder. Milton Evans was the son of well-known Key West shipbuilder Sidney Evans and had learned special woodworking techniques from his father.[259] An African American, Milton Evans along with his eighteen employees constructed homes for both white and black Key Westers. They painstakingly put the nineteenth-century home back together again. When the newly renamed Audubon House was completed, the results were so successful they were almost startling. In fact, it was said that Key West had never before witnessed such an exacting and precise historic restoration. With financial resources, fine construction methods and a team deeply sensitive to Key West's history, the house had been dramatically transformed from a run-down eyesore into a gleaming mansion, as impressive as it had been in Captain Geiger's day.

Although the project had already attracted attention, the Old Island organizers wanted to ensure that everybody knew about it. They decided to create an award, "Old Islander of the Year," and in March 1960 gave the very first one to Mitchell Wolfson. On the evening he received the honor, at a Lions Club dinner with five hundred people in attendance, members

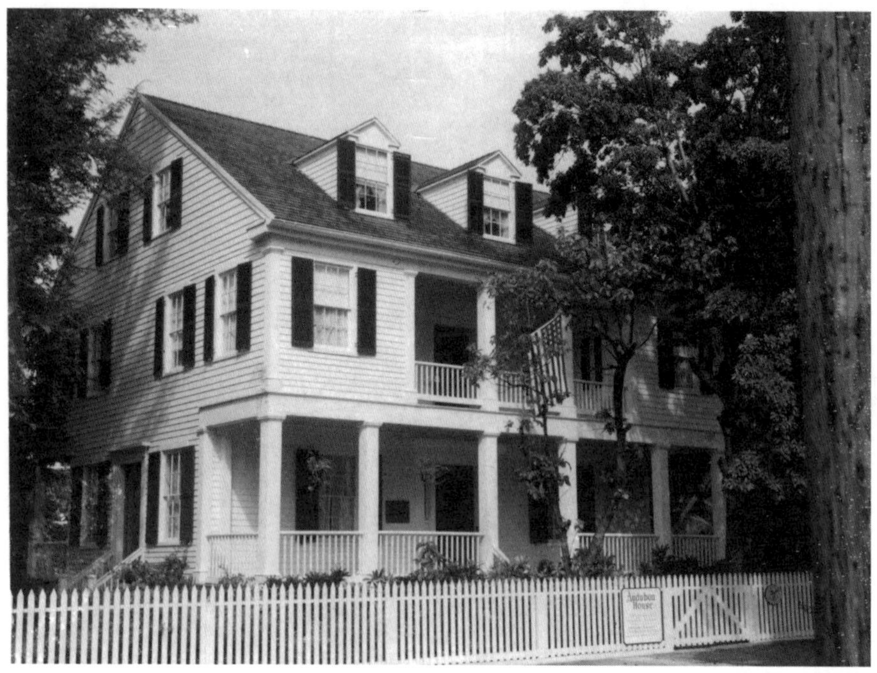

The success of the Audubon House inspired many restoration projects to follow. *Courtesy of the Monroe County Public Library, Key West.*

of the press were there to report on the event. When Mitchell accepted the prize, he thanked the speakers for their "'exaggerated' praise."[260] But in his speech, he added that the job was still unfinished: "I will be extremely happy and rewarded to see a city-wide restoration. This will increase city pride and also improve the economy. Implement your dreams. Make them reality."[261]

It was one of the most exciting social occasions in Key West that year, and that night there was talk of a "Conch Renaissance." Jessie Porter Newton, never one to miss an opportunity, announced that the Old Island Restoration Foundation would soon have a bank account and would gladly be accepting tax-deductible donations.[262] In case anyone doubted that the foundation meant the restoration of the Audubon House as a mere opening act, she confided that the next structure they wished to rescue was the Citadel Lookout Tower at the Martello Galleries. "This is the restoration project I have my heart and soul in," she confessed.[263]

To coincide with the award giving, the foundation organized a tour of homes for what it named the first annual "Old Island Day." Although such tours may be common now, at the time, it was a surprising idea in Key

West. Seven historic homes and offices flung open their doors to hundreds of curious visitors. Unlike certain Conch houses that had grown dilapidated, these buildings were undeniably well maintained, attractive and often furnished with fine antiques. The Newtons showed off the Captain Carey Home, while Mr. and Mrs. Edgar Willing opened up their "old Bahamas type house with gingerbread and a garden."[264] Theatrical producer Walter Starcke invited guests to view his three-room cottage, converted from a children's playhouse.

The majority of people who trooped through these preserved homes were Conchs. (At the time, Key West tourism was in the doldrums.) The aim of Old Island Day was to expose Key Westers to what a well-restored historic home could look like. As a *Miami Herald* article noted, people like Mitchell Wolfson and the tour organizers "don't want neon and CBS. They're for gardens, keeping the old ship's carpenter pegs and letting their grandchildren see what Key West was in its proud days."[265] Although the Old Island Restoration Foundation planned to restore buildings—and did accomplish that—its vision extended further: it wanted to change the prevailing mindset.

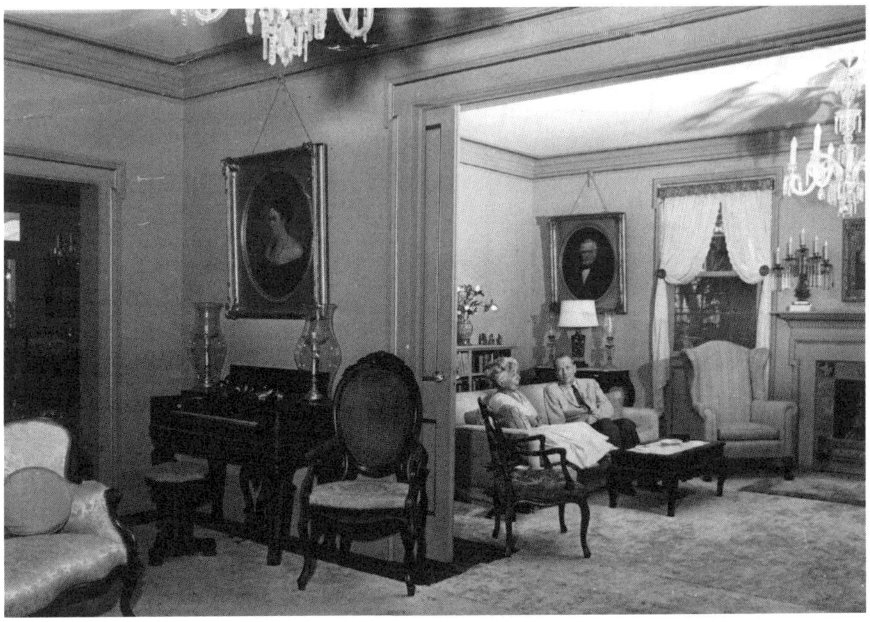

Jessie Porter Newton and Mitchell Wolfson inside her historic home on Caroline Street. *Courtesy of the Monroe County Public Library, Key West.*

While Jessie Porter Newton may have received the most newspaper coverage, she certainly did not work alone. Charter members of the foundation included Key Westers Reta Sawyer, Ruth Holtzberg, Joan Knight, Mary Graham, Margaret Nickerson, May Hill Russell, Walter Starcke, Joseph Pinder and Captain O.A. Sandquist. Interestingly, many of the first and most active participants were women. This was no coincidence. In the late 1950s and early '60s, society did not encourage middle- and upper-middle-class women to work outside the home or run for elected office. Yet volunteerism was socially acceptable, and many talented, intelligent women threw themselves into community service. Historic preservation proved to be a cause where they could effect real change; in cities like Savannah, Georgia, the first steps toward preserving historic structures were undertaken by female-run organizations. The Old Island Restoration Foundation women—along with a sprinkling of male members—likewise led the charge in Key West.

After the success of the Audubon House, the young foundation plunged ahead with more projects. Board members realized that Key West's historic architecture could become a tourist attraction and that tourism and historic preservation could have a mutually beneficial relationship. If tourists came especially to see the old buildings, people would be less likely to tear them down. Moreover, with an influx of tourism dollars, the local economy would prosper, and there would be more money to keep up historic properties. As a result, the Old Island Restoration Foundation set to work creating a master plan both to restore Old Key West and make it welcoming for visitors.

In July 1960, the foundation sent a memo to the island's city commissioners. It requested that the city commission "place the Mallory Dock property in the hands of the Old Island Foundation as legal administrator for the purpose of developing it as a complete, well-rounded tourist attraction." It did not stop there, for it also asked "that a portion of the money now planned for scattered public improvements be used to finance this development." At the time, Mallory Dock, as it was known, was in "deplorable condition." The foundation wished to restore existing buildings there, replace the decrepit old fishing dock, install benches and draw in tourists. The memo, sent by foundation president Reta Sawyer, presents an impeccably argued case:

> *We know from experience that our tourists and winter visitors enjoy our "atmosphere." It is our old buildings that help give us that atmosphere, and it was that same subtle charm that brought the first tourists to Key West—*

and kept them there. It is a highly saleable commodity. Other South Florida cities may surpass us in attractions—but they cannot compete historically, and they completely lack our "foreign" flavor. These are singular, solid-gold assets that we hold in the palm of our hand—yet are not properly developing. Key West has an abundance of what the tourist wants, and—at Mallory Dock—the Old Island Foundation proposes to dramatically present a taste of what the town has to offer, thereby whetting the visitor's appetite and teasing his imagination. If we can attract and interest more visitors and induce them to extend their stay just by a day or so, the increase in annual income to the city would be impressive.[266]

The commissioners may or may not have felt affection for Old Town's buildings, but Reta Sawyer's reasoning was persuasive. Key West very much needed an increase in income. The shift in attitude toward Key West's heritage had started. Elected officials listened. The Mallory Dock project expanded to include surrounding buildings such as a waterfront playhouse, a convention center, a chamber of commerce building and a Spanish walled garden. By the next year, City Manager Basel Crowe expressed in a letter to Reta, "Your continued interest in our city, and city planning is greatly appreciated. We feel that the aims and purposes of Old Island Restoration coincide with the ideas of many, many forward looking people in the City of Key West."[267] Later, when the foundation proposed that Mallory Dock's name be changed to Old Mallory Square, the city obliged.

The foundation's work quickly progressed. In addition to saving specific properties, in short order, Old Island Restoration Foundation members would be operating a Hospitality House for visitors, establishing a self-guided walking tour called the Pelican Path, running annual Old Island Days and lobbying city hall for a reestablished Architectural Board of Review to ensure Old Town's preservation. In 1964, the *Miami Herald* reported, "The new board, in effect, gives the Old Island Restoration Foundation a semi-official voice in construction in the old section of Key West."[268] The busy foundation would raise money to erect historic markers (thereby emphasizing the value of many buildings) and eventually restore Key West's oldest home on Duval Street, known as the Oldest House.

One of its triumphs was to underwrite a Historic American Buildings Survey (HABS) from the National Park Service. Key Westers had not previously taken into account the immense wealth of historic buildings they possessed. The HABS team of a professor and architecture students stayed on the island for three months; they created drawings, photographs and studied a wide range of structures.[269] Their results were exhibited in Key West, but more importantly, the project created an architectural record and provided justification for designating certain buildings official U.S. national landmarks. In other words, the OIRF helped to lay down a bulwark of legislative and regulatory acts that would make the wholesale destruction of historic properties seen in the 1950s a thing of the past.

Even with all these accomplishments, much remained to be done. As the movement for historic preservation spread throughout America, more organizations and individual residents in Key West began to take action. In 1968, for example, David Wolkowsky moved a neglected nineteenth-century building that had once been the P&O Steamship office from one side of Duval Street to the other and used it as the centerpiece for a hip restaurant, Tony's Fish Market. In 1972, Ed Swift, Moe Mosher and Chris Belland formed the Old Town Key West Development, which renovated numerous buildings, among them the Key West Aquarium. The gay community, which had grown up around playwright Tennessee Williams, also started to buy and restore homes and made a striking contribution to the island's preservation.[270] To adequately describe all the people and all the projects that have revived Key West's historic district would take many more pages.

Fortunately, the dream of those engaged residents who gathered in Jessie Porter's back garden decades ago has largely been fulfilled. Key West's architectural treasures will never again be under threat like they were in the 1950s. Yet the work of maintaining antique wooden structures in a tropical seaside climate never ends. Today, the Old Island Restoration Foundation continues its mission.

Notes

Chapter 1

1. Peters, "William Adee Whitehead's Reminiscences," 5.
2. Ibid., 25.
3. Ibid., 24–25.
4. Ibid., 25.
5. Ibid.
6. Texas Navy Association, Charles E. Hawkins Squadron, "Charles Edward Hawkins."
7. Peters, "William Adee Whitehead's Reminiscences," 24.
8. Ibid.
9. In his "Reminiscences," Key West settler William Whitehead recalled that Hawkins was giving a dinner that night in honor of McRea. Although this recollection may be accurate, because it was written forty-eight years after the event and about thirty-eight years after Whitehead left Key West, one may be justified in wondering whether he conflated events.
10. Maynard, "According to Their Capacities and Talents," 51.
11. Peters, "William Adee Whitehead's Reminiscences," 25.
12. Ibid.
13. In another curious twist, Andrew Jackson was a family friend of Algernon Thruston's. Thruston was the man William McRea had previously dueled for the affections of Elizabeth Duval. After he became president in 1829, Jackson appointed Thruston collector of customs for Key West.
14. Andrew Jackson, letter to Richard Keith Call, September 9, 1819.

15. Drake, "Duel!"
16. Ibid.
17. Ibid.
18. Ibid.
19. *Genius of Liberty*, "From Key West," 2.
20. Ibid.
21. Texas Navy Association, Charles E. Hawkins Squadron, "Charles Edward Hawkins."
22. Peters, "William Adee Whitehead's Reminiscences," 25.
23. Texas Navy Association, Charles E. Hawkins Squadron, "Charles Edward Hawkins."
24. Peters, "William Adee Whitehead's Reminiscences," 26.
25. Denham, *Florida Founder William P. DuVal*, 164–65.
26. Black, "Richard Fitzpatrick's South Florida, Part I," 54.
27. Acts of the Legislative Council of the Territory of Florida, "An Act for the Relief of Charles E. Hawkins."
28. Ibid.
29. Texas Navy Association, Charles E. Hawkins Squadron, "Charles Edward Hawkins."
30. Grandadge, "Florida Repeals Anti-Dueling Law."

Chapter 2

31. Black, "Richard Fitzpatrick's South Florida, Part I," 58.
32. Ibid., 54.
33. Burke, *Streets of Key West*, 60.
34. Black, "Richard Fitzpatrick's South Florida, Part I," 54.
35. Ibid., 49.
36. Ibid.
37. Ibid., 56–57.
38. Ibid., 62.
39. Ibid., 64.
40. Ibid., 67.
41. Ibid.
42. Black, "Richard Fitzpatrick's South Florida, Part II," 34.
43. Ibid., 35.
44. At the time, the Miami River region lay in Monroe County.
45. Black, "Richard Fitzpatrick's South Florida, Part II," 37.

46. Hackley, "Diary," 12.
47. Black, "Richard Fitzpatrick's South Florida, Part I," 70.
48. Ibid.
49. Ibid., "Richard Fitzpatrick's South Florida, Part II," 46.
50. Ibid., 47.
51. Ibid., 48.
52. Ibid., 42.
53. This was retaliation for a judgement Cooley had rendered, acquitting men for the murder of an Indian chief. While Cooley was away, his wife, children and the children's tutor were killed.
54. Black, "Richard Fitzpatrick's South Florida, Part I," 40.
55. Bertelli, "Wrecker King of Indian Key."
56. Affidavit of William English, before W.C. Maloney, November 28, 1845.
57. Wilkinson, "General History Indian Key."
58. Ibid.
59. Black, "Richard Fitzpatrick's South Florida, Part II," 48–49.
60. Ibid.
61. Ibid., 49.
62. Hudson, "Beginnings in Dade County," 2.
63. Ibid., 5.
64. Black, "Richard Fitzpatrick's South Florida, Part II," 60.
65. Ibid.
66. Ibid., 63.

Chapter 3

67. Camp, "Captain Brannan's Dilemma," 31.
68. Schmidt, *Florida's Keys and Fevers*, 14.
69. Ogle, *Key West*, 57.
70. Burnett, *Florida's Past*, 2:121.
71. Ibid., 2:123.
72. Camp, "Captain Brannan's Dilemma," 33.
73. Ibid., 35.
74. Ibid., 39.
75. Browne, *Key West*, 177.
76. Although chronicler Jefferson Browne reported that Mulrennan sent the letter to Major French, the date of March suggests Mulrennan wrote to Captain Brannan.

77. Schmidt, *Florida's Keys and Fevers*, 28.
78. Ibid.
79. Ibid., 78.
80. Browne, *Key West*, 97.
81. Schmidt, *Florida's Keys and Fevers*, 78–79.
82. Although today the term "Conch" refers to Florida Keys natives, in the nineteenth century it was usually a nickname for Bahamians living in the Keys. The name may have developed due to the Bahamian predilection for eating conch, an odd-looking mollusk that was not commonly found on American dinner tables at the time.
83. Campbell, *Southern Service on Land & Sea*, 5.
84. Ibid.
85. Ibid., 6.
86. Ibid., 8.
87. Ibid., 9.
88. Ibid.
89. Ibid., 10.
90. Dyer, "Hull of Civil War Sloop."
91. Ibid.
92. Ibid.
93. Campbell, *Southern Service on Land & Sea*, 14.
94. Ibid., 31.
95. National Archives and Records Administration (NARA) Publication M251, Reel 79 of 104, Seventh Infantry, "Compiled Service Records of Confederate Soldiers."
96. Ibid.
97. Ibid., Reel 76.
98. Ibid., Reel 77.
99. Campbell, *Southern Service on Land & Sea*, 169.
100. NARA Publication M251, Reel 78, Seventh Infantry.
101. Joseph Fagan and John T. Lowe had also relocated from Key West before the war, as Jefferson Browne mentioned, "Mr. Joseph Fagan and Mr. John T. Lowe were working in Manatee county and joined their comrades in Tampa."
102. NARA Publication M251, Reel 79.
103. Campbell, *Southern Service on Land & Sea*, 12.
104. Ibid.
105. *Official Records of the Union and Confederate Armies*, ser. 1, vol. 53, chap. LXV, 239–40.

106. Campbell, *Southern Service on Land & Sea*, 34.
107. Ibid., 55.
108. The Keys Confederates born in the Bahamas include Robert Watson (Ragged Island), Samuel Morgan (unidentified Bahamian island), Benjamin Richard Albury (Royal Island), Joseph Simon Bartlum (Green Turtle Cay), William D. Curry (unidentified Bahamian island), Alfred B. Lowe (Green Turtle Cay), John Thomas Lowe (Green Turtle Cay), John W. Russell (Green Turtle Cay), John D. Sands (Ragged Island) and Joseph Henry Moss (unidentified Bahamian island).
109. Saunders, *Race and Class in the Colonial Bahamas*, 8.
110. Ibid., 10.
111. Ibid., 12.
112. University Press of Florida, "Race and Class in the Colonial Bahamas."
113. Keys, "Historians Reveal Secrets."
114. Turner, *From Chattel Slaves to Wage Slaves*, 171.
115. Wells, *Forgotten Legacy*, 11–12.
116. One long volume on this subject already exists in the form of Schmidt, *Florida's Keys and Fever*, vol. 3.
117. Campbell, *Southern Service on Land & Sea*, 162.

Chapter 4

118. Taylor and Day, "Adderley House," registration form, National Register of Historic Places, 3.
119. Ibid., 2.
120. The inlet (called Rachel Creek) was once open to Florida Bay, but the access point was filled in during the 1950s.
121. Taylor and Day, "Adderley House," registration form, 4.
122. Ibid.
123. Gall and Veit, *Archaeologies of African American Life*, 63.
124. Ibid.
125. Until 1912, the train only went as far south as Knight's Key Dock in the Middle Keys. From late January 1912 and onward, Adderley Town residents could travel south to Key West.
126. Atkins, "Time Stands Still for Oldest Keys House."
127. Ibid.

Chapter 5

128. Grosscup, "Flagler's Folly."
129. *St. Louis Globe Democrat*, "Lessons from Panama Taught in Florida."
130. Wilkinson, "1907 'Key West Extension Scare.'"
131. Ibid.
132. Florida East Coast Railway Construction Evaluation Report, Section 4, June 30, 1907–June 30, 1908.
133. Wilkinson, "1907 'Key West Extension Scare.'"
134. Ibid.
135. Ibid.
136. Like several other articles in William Krome's scrapbooks, there is no indication of the newspaper in which this piece originally appeared.
137. Wilkinson, "1907 'Key West Extension Scare.'"
138. Florida East Coast Railway Construction Evaluation Report, Section 4.
139. Wilkinson, "1907 'Key West Extension Scare.'"
140. *Key West Citizen*, "Work Resumed on Trumbo Island."
141. Wilkinson, "Early Evolution of the Key West Extension."

Chapter 6

142. Bertelli and Wilkinson, *Key Largo*, 44.
143. Ibid.
144. Ibid., 68.
145. *Key West Citizen*, "Colored Woman Caught on Road."
146. Kerstein, *Key West on the Edge*, 57.
147. Woolf, "Rum, Hookers and Smuggling."
148. *Key West Citizen*, "Rodriguez Raided."
149. Garnett, "Rum-Running in the Economy of the Keys."
150. Ibid.
151. Ibid.
152. Ibid.
153. Ibid.
154. Ibid.
155. *Key West Citizen*, "Officers Make Haul of Liquor."
156. Ibid., "Customs Officials of This City."
157. Ibid.

158. Ibid., "Only Six Cases Grow."
159. Kennedy, "Captain Antonio," 2.
160. Ibid.
161. Ibid.
162. Ibid.
163. Smith, "'Deacon' Recalls Key Rum Runs."
164. Ibid.
165. Ibid.
166. Kennedy, "Captain Antonio," 2.
167. Ibid., 3.
168. Ibid.
169. Sally J. Ling, "Marie Waite."
170. Willoughby, *Rum War at Sea*, 119.
171. *Miami Herald*, "Held for Liquor."
172. Willoughby, *Rum War at Sea*, 119.
173. Ibid.
174. Ibid., 120.
175. *Miami Herald*, "Marie Waite Saez Held on Dry Charge."
176. Ibid.

Chapter 7

177. Key Largo Angler's Club, "About KLAC."
178. Wilkinson, "North Key Largo."
179. Ibid., "History of the Overseas Highway."
180. Ibid.
181. Parks, *George Merrick*, 309.
182. Ibid., 309–10.
183. Bertelli and Wilkinson, *Key Largo*, 48.
184. Parks, *George Merrick*, 310.
185. Wilkinson, "North Key Largo."
186. Layman with Rivett, *Selected Letters of Dashiell Hammett*, 83.
187. Ibid., 84–85.
188. Ibid., 85.
189. Ward, *Lost Detective*, 161.
190. Wilkinson, "North Key Largo."
191. Ibid.
192. Bertelli and Wilkinson, *Key Largo*, 48.

193. Parks, *George Merrick*, 304.
194. Ibid.
195. Ibid.
196. Ibid., 305.
197. Ibid., 306.
198. Ibid., 308.
199. Ibid., 316.
200. Ibid.
201. Wilkinson, "Hurricane History Homepage," Florida Keys History Museum.
202. Parks, *George Merrick*, 316.

Chapter 8

203. Link, *Sea Diver*, 11.
204. Albritton and Wilkinson, *Marathon*, 75.
205. Ibid., 19.
206. Ibid., 19–20.
207. Ibid., 8.
208. Ibid., 10.
209. Peterson, "Last Voyage of the H.M.S. 'Looe,'" 4.
210. Ibid., 77.
211. Link, *Sea Diver*, 5.
212. Ibid., 7.
213. Ibid., 5.
214. Ibid., 9.
215. Ibid., 13.
216. Ibid., 75.
217. Bertelli, "Art McKee."
218. Ibid.
219. Wilkinson, "Art 'Silver Bar' McKee."
220. Ibid.
221. Link, *Sea Diver*, 91.
222. Ibid., 92.
223. Wilkinson, "Art 'Silver Bar' McKee."

Chapter 9

224. Gold, "Figure Behind the Fan."
225. Ibid.
226. Ediger, "Sally Rand."
227. Caemmerer, *Houses of Key West*, 84.
228. Daniels, "Sally Rand."
229. Ibid.
230. Ibid.
231. Wood, *Wicked Women of Missouri*, 100.
232. Ibid.
233. Tim Estiloz, interview with Bettie Page.
234. Foster, *Real Bettie Page*, 94.
235. Ibid.
236. Ibid., 94–95.
237. Ibid., 95.
238. Larkin, *Bettie Page*.
239. Foster, *Real Bettie Page*, 95.
240. Ibid.
241. Guerra, "Interview Unravels Key West Lore."
242. Ibid.
243. Ibid.
244. Ibid.

Chapter 10

245. O'Hara, "Heritage House Museum Closes."
246. Ibid.
247. Voltz, "Mrs. Jessie P. Newton."
248. Ibid.
249. Ibid.
250. Williams, *Florida Keys*, 142.
251. Hambright, interviewed by Laura Albritton.
252. Howard, "Tourism Renaissance in Key West."
253. Ibid.
254. Ibid.
255. Williams, *Florida Keys*, 142.
256. O'Hara, "Heritage House Museum Closes."

257. Hambright, interviewed by Laura Albritton.
258. Ibid.
259. Sawyer and Wells-Bowie, *Key West*, 33.
260. Porter, "Historic Interest Growing."
261. Ibid.
262. Ibid.
263. Ibid.
264. Porter and Rabon, "Key West Opens Old Island Homes."
265. Ibid.
266. Old Island Foundation Inc. to Members of the Board of City Commissioners, July 6, 1960.
267. Basel E. Crowe to Mrs. Paul Sawyer, July 20, 1961.
268. Ediger, "City Action Scheduled for Today."
269. *Key West Citizen*, "Historic Bldg. Study Results."
270. Hambright, interviewed by Laura Albritton.

Bibliography

Acts of the Legislative Council of the Territory of Florida, 1831. "An Act for the Relief of Charles E. Hawkins." http://ufdc.ufl.edu/UF00073402/00009.

Albritton, Laura, and Jerry Wilkinson. *Marathon: The Middle Keys*. Charleston, SC: Arcadia Publishing, 2016.

Atkins, Katie. "Time Stands Still for Oldest Keys House Outside Key West." *The Keynoter*, May 29, 2017.

Bertelli, Brad. "Art McKee, the Tip of the Iceberg." *The Reporter*, January 23, 2015. http://www.flkeysnews.com/living/article79613742.html.

———. "The Wrecker King of Indian Key." *The Reporter*, June 21, 2013. http://www.flkeysnews.com/living/article79610767.html.

Bertelli, Brad, and Jerry Wilkinson. *Key Largo*. Charleston, SC: Arcadia Publishing, 2012.

Black, Hugo L., III. "Richard Fitzpatrick's South Florida, 1822–1840, Part I: Key West Phase." *Tequesta* 40 (1980): 47–77.

———. "Richard Fitzpatrick's South Florida, 1822–1840, Part II: Fitzpatrick's Miami River Plantation." *Tequesta* 41 (1981): 33–68.

Browne, Jefferson B. *Key West: The Old and the New*. St. Augustine, FL: Record Company, 1912.

Burke, J. Wills. *The Streets of Key West: A History through Street Names*. Sarasota, FL: Pineapple Press, 2014.

Burnett, Gene M. *Florida's Past*. Vol. 2, *People and Events that Shaped the State*. Sarasota, FL: Pineapple Press, 1988.

Caemmerer, Alex. *Houses of Key West*. Sarasota, FL: Pineapple Press, 1992.

Camp, Vaughan, Jr. "Captain Brannan's Dilemma: Key West 1861." *Tequesta* 20 (1960): 31–43.

Campbell, R. Thomas, ed. *Southern Service on Land & Sea: The Wartime Journal of Robert Watson, CSA/CSN*. Knoxville: University of Tennessee Press, 2002.

Clubbs, Occie. "Stephen Russell Mallory." *Florida Historical Quarterly* 25, no. 3 (1947): 221–45, 295–318.

Crowe, Basel E., to Mrs. Paul Sawyer, Chairman, Old Island Restoration Foundation, Key West, Florida, July 20, 1961. Monroe Country Library Archives, Key West, Florida.

Daniels, Lee A. "Sally Rand, Whose Fan Dancing Shocked Country, Is Dead at 75." *New York Times*, September 1, 1979.

Denham, James J. *Florida Founder William P. DuVal: Frontier Bon Vivant*. Columbia: University of South Carolina Press, 2015.

Denham, James L., and Keith L. Huneycutt, eds. *Echoes from a Distant Frontier: The Brown Sisters' Correspondence from Antebellum Florida*. Columbia: University of South Carolina Press, 2004.

Dodd, Dorothy. "Jacob Housman of Indian Key." *Tequesta* 8 (1948): 3–19.

Drake, Ross. "Duel!" *Smithsonian Magazine*, March 2004. http://www.smithsonianmag.com/history/duel-104161025.

Dyer, Elisabeth. "Hull of Civil War Sloop Likely Found in Tampa River." *Tampa Bay Times*, May 21, 2008.

Ediger, Don. "City Action Scheduled for Today." *Miami Herald*, December 3, 1964.

———. "Sally Rand." *Miami Herald*, August 20, 1967.

English, William. Affidavit of William English, before W.C. Maloney, November 28, 1845. Jerry Wilkinson Papers.

Estiloz, Tim. Interview with Bettie Page. *Real Life*. NBC, 1996.

Florida Department of Military Affairs. *Florida Soldiers: CSA 6th, 7th Florida Infantry, 1st Florida Cavalry*. St. Augustine, FL: State Arsenal, St. Francis Barracks, 1990. http://ufdc.ufl.edu/UF00047676/00001.

Florida East Coast Railway Construction Evaluation Report, Section 4, June 30, 1907, to June 30, 1908. Jerry Wilkinson Papers.

Foster, Richard. *The Real Bettie Page: The Truth About the Queen of the Pinups*. New York: Citadel Press, 1997.

Gall, Michael J., and Richard F. Veit. *Archaeologies of African American Life in the Upper Mid Atlantic*. Tuscaloosa: University of Alabama Press, 2017.

Garnett, Burt. "Rum-Running in the Economy of the Keys." *Martello*, February 5, 1967.

Genius of Liberty 31, no. 25. "From Key West" (June 27, 1829).

Gold, Sylviane. "The Figure Behind the Fan: Celebrating Sally Rand." *New York Times*, June 27, 2004.

Grandadge, Johnathan. "Florida Repeals Anti-Dueling Law (1832)." Florida Memory Blog, February 8, 2012. http://www.floridamemory.com/blog/2012/02/08/florida-repeals-anti-dueling-law-1832.

Grosscup, Luann. "'Flagler's Folly': An 'Overseas' Railroad to Key West." *Chicago Tribune*, March 8, 1998.

Guerra, John L. "Interview Unravels Key West Lore." *Key West Citizen*, July 18, 2010.

Hackley, William. "Diary of William Hackley." *Florida Keys Sea Heritage Journal* 22, no. 4 (2012): 12.

Hambright, Tom, Senior Librarian—Florida History, Monroe County Library. Interviewed by Laura Albritton, Key West, Florida, October 30, 2017.

Howard, Elizabeth. "A Tourism Renaissance in Key West." *Washington Post*, March 6, 1977.

Hudson, F.M. "Beginnings in Dade County." *Tequesta* 1, no. 3 (1943): 1–35.

Jackson, Andrew, letter to Richard Keith Call, September 9, 1819. State Archives of Florida, Call Family Papers, Box 5, Folder 5, Item 4. https://www.floridamemory.com/items/show/181304?id=2.

Kennedy, Stetson. "Captain Antonio." Transcription of interview, Key West, Florida, 1938.

Kerstein, Robert. *Key West on the Edge: Inventing the Conch Republic*. Gainesville: University Press of Florida, 2012.

Key Largo Angler's Club. "About KLAC." http://www.klac.org/About-KLAC.aspx.

Keys, David. "Historians Reveal Secrets of UK Gun-Running which Lengthened the American Civil War by Two Years." *The Independent*, June 23, 2014. http://www.independent.co.uk/news/science/archaeology/historians-reveal-secrets-of-uk-gun-running-which-lengthened-the-american-civil-war-by-two-years-9557937.html.

Key West Citizen. "Colored Woman Caught on Road with Wet Goods." December 12, 1932.

———. "Customs Officials of This City Make Rich Bacardi Haul." February 17, 1927

———. "Historic Bldg. Study Results Will Be Shown." September 7, 1967.

———. "Officers Make Haul of Liquor." September 29, 1932.

———. "Only Six Cases Grow from Dry Raids on Friday." April 23, 1927.

———. “Rodriguez Raided.” Notes of the Passing Day, March 7, 1927.

———. “Work Resumed on Trumbo Island.” September 11, 1909.

Larkin, Carlos. *Bettie Page: The Girl in the Leopard Print Bikini*. Art directed by Cristyan Cadena, 2004. Multicom Entertainment Group, streaming video.

Layman, Richard, with Julie M. Rivett, eds. *Selected Letters of Dashiell Hammett, 1921–1960*. Washington, D.C.: Counterpoint, 2001.

Link, Marion Clayton. *Sea Diver*. New York: Rinehart & Company, 1958.

Maynard, Jackson Wilder. “According to Their Capacities and Talents: Attorneys in Tallahassee during the Territorial Period.” Master’s thesis, Florida State University, 2004.

Miami Herald. “Held for Liquor.” September 21, 1930.

———. “Marie Waite Saez Held on Dry Charge.” May 27, 1931.

Monroe County Library Archives, Key West, Florida.

National Archives and Records Administration. Seventh Infantry, “Compiled Service Records of Confederate Soldiers Who Served in Organizations From the State of Florida.” Publication M251, Reels 76–79 of 104. http://www.civilwarmicrofilm.com/site/viewer/thumbnailViewer.php?imageNumber=1864&reelREF=79.

Official Records of the Union and Confederate Armies, 1861–1865. Ser. 1, vol. 53, chap. LXV, 239–40.

Ogle, Maureen. *Key West: History of an Island of Dreams*. Gainesville: University Press of Florida, 2003.

O’Hara, Timothy. “Heritage House Museum Closes.” *Key West Citizen*, April 16, 2010.

Parks, Arva Moore. *George Merrick: Son of the South Wind*. Gainesville: University Press of Florida, 2015.

Peters, Thelma, ed. “William Adee Whitehead’s Reminiscences of Key West.” *Tequesta* 25 (1965): 3–42.

Peterson, Mendel L. “The Last Voyage of the H.M.S. ‘Looe.’” *Smithsonian Miscellaneous Collections*. Vol. 131. Washington, D.C.: Smithsonian Institution, 1958.

Porter, Fred. “Historic Interest Growing.” *Miami Herald*, March 20, 1960.

Porter, Fred, and Florence Rabon. “Key West Opens Old Island Homes.” *Miami Herald*, March 20, 1960.

Sally J. Ling—Florida’s History Detective. “Marie Waite—‘Spanish Marie.’” https://sallyjling.org/marie-waite-spanish-marie.

Saunders, Gail. *Race and Class in the Colonial Bahamas, 1880–1960*. Gainesville: University Press of Florida, 2016.

Sawyer, Norma Jean, and LaVerne Wells-Bowie. *Key West*. Black America Series. Charleston, SC: Arcadia Publishing, 2002.

Sawyer, Reta. The Old Island Foundation Inc. to Members of the Board of City Commissioners, Key West, Florida, July 6, 1960. Monroe Country Library Archives, Key West, Florida.

Schmidt, Lewis G. *Florida's Keys and Fevers: The Civil War in Florida, a Military History*. Vol. 3. Allentown, PA: Lewis G. Schmidt, 1992.

Smith, Anne. "'Deacon' Recalls Keys Rum Runs." *Miami Herald*, October 22, 1966.

St. Louis Globe Democrat. "Lessons from Panama Taught in Florida." April 14, 1907.

Taylor, Tulie W., and Jane Day. "The Adderley House," registration form. National Register of Historic Places, August 5, 1992.

Texas Navy Association, Charles E. Hawkins Squadron. "Charles Edward Hawkins (c. 1802–37)." https://texasnavygalveston.org/charles-edward-hawkins-1802-37.

Turner, Mary, ed. *From Chattel Slaves to Wage Slaves: The Dynamics of Labour Bargaining in the Americas*. Bloomington: Indiana University Press, 1995.

Underwood, Rodman L. *Stephen Russell Mallory: A Biography of the Confederate Navy Secretary and United States Senator*. Jefferson, NC: McFarland, 2005.

University Press of Florida. "Race and Class in the Colonial Bahamas, 1880–1960." http://upf.com/book.asp?id=SAUND002.

Viele, John. *The Florida Keys: A History of the Pioneers*. Sarasota, FL: Pineapple Press, 1996.

Voltz, Jeanne. "Mrs. Jessie P. Newton Is a House Collector." *Miami Herald*, March 9, 1960.

Ward, Nathan. *The Lost Detective: Becoming Dashiell Hammett*. New York: Bloomsbury, 2015.

Wells, Sharon. *Forgotten Legacy: Blacks in Nineteenth Century Key West*. Key West, FL: Historic Key West Preservation Board, 1982.

Wilkinson, Jerry. "Art 'Silver Bar' McKee." Florida Keys History Museum. http:// http://www.keyshistory.org/Art_McKee.html.

———. "The Early Evolution of the Key West Extension." Florida Keys History Museum. http://www.keyshistory.org/Evolution-Of-Key-West-Extension.html.

———. "General History Indian Key: Housman Period (1831–1840)." Florida Keys History Museum. http://www.keyshistory.org/IK-general-history1.html.

———. "History of Marathon." Florida Keys History Museum. http://www.keyshistory.org/marathon.html.

———. "History of the Overseas Highway." Florida Keys History Museum. http://www.keyshistory.org/osh.html.

———. "Hurricane History Homepage." Florida Keys History Museum. http://www.keyshistory.org/35-hurr-homepage.html.

———. "The 1907 'Key West Extension Scare.'" Presentation, Historical Preservation Society of the Upper Keys meeting, April 2011.

———. "North Key Largo." Florida Keys History Museum. http:// www.keyshistory.org/nokeylargopage2.html.

Williams, Joy. *The Florida Keys: A History & Guide*. 10th ed. New York: Random House, 2003.

Willoughby, Malcolm F. *Rum War at Sea*. Washington, D.C.: Treasury Department, U.S. Coast Guard, 1964.

Wood, Larry. *Wicked Women of Missouri*. Charleston, SC: The History Press, 2016.

Woolf, Christopher. "Rum, Hookers and Smuggling: The Secret Story of the Last Presidential Visit to Cuba." Public Radio International, National Public Radio, March 17, 2016. http://www.pri.org/stories/2016—3-17/rum-hookers-and-smuggling.

Index

About the Authors

Fifth-generation Floridian Laura Albritton is a writer, book reviewer and writing teacher. Her work has appeared in publications such as the *Miami Herald*, *Sculpture* magazine, *Harvard Review* and the *Florida Keys Weekly*, while her award-winning short fiction has been published in many literary journals. She wrote the travel book *Miami for Families* (University Press of Florida) and coauthored *Marathon: The Middle Keys* and *Key West's Duval Street* (Arcadia Publishing) with Jerry Wilkinson. Laura holds a degree in comparative literature from Columbia and an MFA in creative writing from the University of Miami.

Fourth-generation Floridian Jerry Wilkinson arrived in Key West in 1947. He served in the U.S. Air Force for twenty-four years before operating his own business. For decades, Jerry has researched and documented Florida Keys history, particularly that of the Upper Keys. He has contributed to books, films and television programs and created an extensive Keys history website (www.keyshistory.org). Jerry is president of the Historical Preservation Society of the Upper Keys and serves on the boards of the Historic Florida Keys Foundation and the Florida Keys History and Discovery Center. Jerry's previous books include *Key Largo* and *Islamorada*, coauthored with Brad Bertelli.